"Just sit there right now—don't do a thing, just rest.
For your separation from God, from love,
Is the hardest work in this world.
Let me bring you trays of food and something that you like to drink.
You can use my soft words as a cushion for your head."

—Hafiz

CONTENTS

INTRODUCTION

This book is offered as an invitation to the most important of human undertakings: communication with the Source of life and love. Throughout the challenging mortal journey, we are looking for navigational tools—a plumb line, a compass: "Why am I here and how do I travel through this life, bordered by its twin mysteries of birth and death?" There are countless explanations for what is happening in this passage, but what we really need is compassionate personal guidance as we navigate this often baffling terrain. Wouldn't it be wonderful if wise helpers were constantly available to each one of us? More and more people are discovering that such help is not only possible but also quite readily available. It is the purpose of this book to offer a template for attuning to loving spiritual conversation. Here is one person's journey: here are messages that offer compassionate enlightenment along the way. It is hoped that the reader will use these messages and exercises as an entryway into their own divine conversation.

Like you, I am a fragile human being trying to find meaning along a mysterious path. I do not claim any particular spiritual gift. Early trauma awakened in me a lifelong desire to wrestle light out of darkness. Through creativity I've tried to inspire transformation—as a portrait artist I created sketches of "enemy" faces as a gesture towards awakening global consciousness, and as an actress I enacted the inspiring words of an Auschwitz victim who saw light beyond the horror. But the spiritual calling has eventually led me into the innermost caverns of my heart. It now seems to me that this is the real place where enlightenment begins. I have been waiting on inner guidance, and the more I wait the clearer it is that the waiting is the most fruitful pursuit of all.

I think there are innumerable unseen presences here to help us. (At last I do believe this, though for decades I've danced in and out of being sure.) They are here. And our relationship with them—those I think of as spiritual messengers—is apparently our lifeline in this material world. What we see, hear and touch perishes: this body, this chair, this home. But the sweet conversation with unseen helpers is eternal.

The conversations in this book speak of the human dream which sometimes feels like a nightmare. In this historical moment we are awakening from the dream, and the waking is both confusing and infinitely rewarding. We begin to see the world's history of glory and travail as a child's attempt at love, a thirsty person begging for water. We have seen "through a glass darkly" and now we will see face to face. What an amazing time this is … and how challenging. At a time when global institutions crumble, the earth quakes and waters rise, we are asked to be still, go inward, and seek the Lover of our souls. We are asked to run in the wrong direction.

The thing that waits for us here inside is the only real thing there is: the Abiding Conversation. When all else falls away there is only this—the eternal dance of lovers. The path is here, the doorway is within. The time is now.

Jane Smith Bernhardt

A STILL CUP

"For God to make love, for the divine alchemy to work,
The pitcher needs a still cup.
Why ask Hafiz to say anything more about your most vital requirement?"
—Hafiz

What is the Conversation and how does it begin?

Most of human suffering may be traced to false identification: we think that who we truly are is this body which we carry for a relatively short time. Our brains, composed of mortal substance, can grasp neither death nor immortality. To reorient our consciousness with the Source of our eternal being is a delicate and sacred process. Without this reorientation we will continue to be defined by the success or failure of this body, which in any case will disintegrate. What part of us is capable of making the leap into eternal consciousness?

There seems to be a place in each of us that yearns for the missing connection with one I think of as the Lover of our soul. Without this connection we are adrift in an incomprehensible universe. The good news is that the Lover is also seeking communion with us. Right here and now we may begin to open ourselves to the sweetest conversation there is.

My advice is to begin in any way that suits you. Remember: this is the delicious, divine encounter that we are seeking. It will help to release any sense of obligation. What do you enjoy? Some will wish to use traditional methods of meditation—to sit comfortably with a straight back and focus on a mantra or the breath, allowing the thoughts that come into the mind to be noticed and dispersed, like cloud formations that pass across the sky. Some will find it helpful to read a passage of spiritual text and allow an inspiring message to gently carry them into a place of peace where divine presence is felt. Some may desire to write a question on a pad of paper or a journal and wait quietly in the expectation that an answer will come. Some may invoke the many names of God that allow their souls to soften and receive. These names are like bars of music through which the unnameable may come.

The place that is harder to describe is the other end of the conversation. How do we know when the thought that comes into our mind is from a loving spiritual source, and how do we know when we are making it up? My advice is to abandon such questioning. For the mind steeped in materialistic thinking, there will be no satisfactory answer. Here is a maze that will only waste our time. If the voice is loving, if it feels as warm and familiar as a gentle embrace, then receive it with gratitude. Gradually you will learn to recognize when Love is speaking.

Waiting

Faith

I lay out my dry seeds in expectation. Shivering in the cold I pour them sloppily into the feeder and go back inside to wait.

Who would want my humble offerings? Who would hear the opening and closing of the door, the crumbling on snow, the clatter of scattering seeds?

I wait, seeing nothing but the stark horizon. Will they come? Who will come?

For some time, I have enjoyed spending significant parts of many mornings in quiet. The sense has been one of an invitation to wait in stillness, and nothing else has been stirring my passion—no great work or vision. It is often a battle to feel all right about this inactivity, especially when there are so many pressing material needs outside the door of my little room. But the sense has persisted that this is the right pursuit. And often I am quietly guided to open this or that book to a passage which builds upon a theme begun the day before. It has become clear to me that I am receiving guidance, and I cherish that.

Sometimes, in the midst of my quiet, the sense comes of a longer message ... a conversation. I have begun to record these in my journal as they come. Though at times personal, they convey deep lessons about the nature of life and truth.

I cannot name with any certainty the source of the messages I receive. By its very nature, the source is mysterious. I would not argue if you said, "This is your own deep wisdom speaking," or, "This is your guardian angel." Remaining open-minded and open-hearted seems to me the widest net that can be cast, because I do not know the parameters of the Unseen. When it comes to the nature of creation and eternal life I know so little. That is why I am asking. That is why I am seeking with all my heart.

Perhaps I ask: "What do you wish to say?" And after a pause that may be long or short an answer may begin to form in my mind, and I simply record the words as they come....

Be still. I am always with you. You are learning to be with me. Breathe in the stillness. Let it be.

How can I describe the way these thoughts come? They are stirrings of the heart. In the beginning there were long silences as I waited, with my cat in my lap and my cup of tea. And I began to simply enjoy the waiting. From time to time a thought or inspiration would come that felt like a loving gift whispered into my soul, and I would record it in my journal and continue to listen. The longer messages included in this book came much later, when I had learned to trust a certain attunement to loving unseen presence. But even now I often ask, "Am I forming the words faithfully? Am I making them up?"

Sometimes I see myself as a beggar waiting before God's door. A sense of Presence comes, warming me. The still silent voice says: *"Receive my gifts, beloved. Receive me. I love you."* It is then that I remember—just as the leaves lean into sunshine for their nourishment—my soul is longing for this nurture, and it is always near.

Each day some light is offering itself to me, and each day my little job is to discover it. It isn't in any sense loud or obtrusive. I realize I need to incline my heart into it. This voice cannot be rightly heard with my mind—some deeper part of me must receive this form of speech. The real impediment seems to be the fear of believing this—that I have heaven on earth if I wish it. And if I can experience it, even for a moment, it is available to everyone at all times.

1,000 Reasons

When you decide to have 'quiet time,' there will be 1,000 reasons not to: too tired, too jumpy, too much to do, a phone-call to answer, an e-mail to send. Every day new reasons will be invented ... until you recognize them for what they are—a smokescreen. Of course, if you are a parent with small children or you are ill and cannot focus, there may be no choice in the matter. But try anyway, if only for a minute. Say: "In this moment I am seeking the creator of all-that-is (Loving Source, God, Allah, Yahweh…). In this moment I am seeking to align myself with the loving energy of the universe." Use the language that best suits you. And in that moment allow yourself to be available to this alone.

We are not looking for something magical or supernatural. Indeed, the fabric of our being is what we might call Cosmic Consciousness. We are stilling ourselves. Like pools of water clouded by the detritus of busy activity, we find the ground of our being more clearly in stillness. Then, as the debris settles, what is most natural begins to reveal itself to us. It is not necessary to receive messages—it is enough to begin to be aware of a kind of peace and clarity, when immediate concerns slip away. Remember in this new cosmology that less is more. Stillness is powerful. Gentle observation is fruitful. Open to unseen grace and let divine helpers do the work.

Exercise for the Reader:

Center yourself for a moment in comfortable stillness. Breathe, relax, and notice the sounds and sensations in your environment. Sink into this stillness as if it were a safe cocoon, and feel the gentle fullness of the air around you as you resolve to simply wait upon the Source of life.

Ask yourself: "What am I looking for?" You may use the space on these pages or in your journal to write down your questions and your thoughts. The Bible says, "Seek me and you shall find me, if you seek me with all your heart." What is it that you are seeking with all your heart? Write (or draw) until you feel that you have expressed what is in your heart, and hold this as your intention: "This is what I am seeking." This will help you to align with your soul's intention in this life. It will help you to awaken the voice of your heart.

... Ask yourself: "What am I looking for?" You may use the space on these pages or in your journal to write down your questions and your thoughts.

THE OPEN DOOR

"...the ability to draw consciously upon nonphysical guidance and assistance, to communicate with a nonphysical teacher, is a treasure that cannot be described, a treasure beyond words and value."
—Gary Zukov, *Seat of the Soul*

I come to the morning quiet time with all of my humanity. Inevitably, my mind begins by dredging up its own chaos, concerns and heavy thoughts. I think: "How can God's voice possibly break through all of this?" Spiritual reading often helps to open a portal, and I have found myself grazing all over, from the Bible to the Persian mystics, from Lao Tzu to the most current New Age explorations: there are so many doorways. Anything that expands my heart seems to do the trick. I open myself to whatever word or passage speaks to me, and then I let it fill me. I wait, trying to be patient with the nervous fear that there is nothing here but my own convoluted isolation. Eventually something seems to shift a bit: my heart softens and somehow I know—in my still, subtle parts—that I am not alone.

In my journal I record my thoughts or questions and wait for that sense of inspiration which seems to arrive in the form of a sweet unbidden thought. I try to record the thought without judgment, just as it comes.

Expectation

My unseen friends: often I come to this quiet time, and I just seem to wait and wait. Will you speak to me about this?

(After some time of quiet expectation, a small thought arises from the emptiness. As I record the words in my journal, the message continues....)

It is a sweet time, the waiting. What is happening? Sifting thoughts in fragments, some charged feelings: anger, sadness, self-criticism. But like clouds that gather and disperse you observe them. You are not the clouds. But you see them and feel them and let the air blow through them, waiting....

It is a bit like expecting to meet someone at a terminal, when one is unsure of just who that person is, or even if they will appear—but one knows that this meeting is the important one, the central thing in the whole journey. Without it one is passing time. And with it, through it, one is connected to the grid of love and meaning. One is enlivened: one's being makes sense. So waiting is the least one can do.

In the morning you gather and receive light. It is a quiet task. As the light comes in, it may illuminate areas of sadness, fatigue or discouragement. Remember, it is the Light that does the work! You carry light, listen to it, serve its needs ... but not independently. It is a relational dance in which Light leads and you take up the rhythm with a willing step. Try not to judge yourself. We never judge you. We are well aware of the heaviness of this planet. Remember that to receive and hold this heaviness is a form of spiritual service. Holding the darkness or the density in light ... produces Light. Holding it in love ... produces Love. Only light can produce Light; only love is the way to Love.

Please always remember that we are here with you, seeking and serving in Love.

All Will Be Well

It seems that on most mornings I wake up with gnarly feelings: guilt, anxiety, negativity. What do I do when I wake up with this darkness?

Center yourself in Oneness and in our conversation. Remember who you are: a being both human and divine. The mortal self presents myriad challenges, even as your immortal being calls you into the great eternal dance. This is not an easy path to navigate. Every morning we begin again at the beginning.

It will not always be this way—a time will come before long when you will not be lost in forgetting. You can help this day along with your awareness: we are here together in the path of Light.

I could use some specific directions on what this entails.

The best practice will be an easy one. When you become aware of the inner voice of doom and gloom, address it kindly but directly: "I want to remind you that all is well—things are not as they seem. Light is everywhere; Love is unstoppable; Grace abounds. We are not alone: armies of ancestors and spirit helpers are healing this planet...." Let the words come to you and enjoy the creative process of imagining new realities. Like creating a pretty picture or poem, or talking to a child. Lighten the discourse with hope, beauty and inspiration.

Remember that those old voices are nothing more than dust, or the vapors of a bad dream. Yes, great horrors have been perpetrated on this earth, but what remains now of all that darkness? Nothing but memories, and even those are fading. The greatest evils are temporary and soon transformed. There is no permanent home for darkness in creation. All is transmuted into Light.

Now is the time of alchemy where base metals are forged into purer stuff. The fire needs to be hot. The alchemist, sure of her purpose, wears a smile of confidence: "All will be well, and all manner of things will be well." (Julian of Norwich)

Practice

I am tired and asking for guidance today. Be with me. Please speak to me.

We are here.

Do you have words for me today?

Love is pushing through the tired places, the cracks, renewing the self, feasting on the light that dances between elements. This is the song of life, the music of the spheres, the great "OM." Begin to feed on this sound even before you are able to hear or discern its presence everywhere. Awareness will increase with practice.

How shall I practice?

Open your palm, face upward, relaxed. Let your fingers gently "breathe".... Feel that they are porous—not impenetrable, as you would imagine metal or rock to be—but sentient, receptive, taking in and releasing breath or energy from the surrounding air. Feel the 'being-sense' of your fingers: what are they experiencing?

Cold, tingly ... quiet, receptive ... simple, physical .... Am I missing something?

They are conduits: simple vessels. Now send them love.

(pause) They seem to feel a bit fuller, better ... I perceive them differently....

Could it be said that the body is made up of a combination of elements that conduct energy?

Yes. I see that.

So that is a very simple function of the body—to conduct energy.

Yes.

It conducts energy for a time and then it dies.

Yup.

At one level then, this is the story of the body.

This body is Jane.

Yes. Jane is in this body. Jane is Source perceiving itself from within this body.

This feels a little heavy for me right now. My head is pounding a bit. I don't know if I want to parse Self. Can you make it simpler?

Think of yourself, body and soul, as a vessel that can hold energy in the form of light and hope and love as well as fear and hatred and despair.

This I have experienced.

You may practice holding light: practice small helpings of joy, humor, hope....

This I can try.

For the Reader:

I love the notion of a spiritual practice, because it makes me think of a child skipping rope, or an actor who isn't yet quite sure of his lines. What is implied is that this thing is never finished or perfected: it is a process, begun anew each day. What felt so good yesterday doesn't fit today. Only in sweet communion with the Beloved will my soul find its way.

What is your practice today? What is your heart asking? Use the space below to write your feelings and desires. And then patiently wait. Be willing to wait for five minutes. That is not a long time. Remember: you do not know just what you are waiting for. This is may be a new experience—enter into it with gentleness and patience. Keep your expectations to a minimum: simply notice what is happening, and treasure these moments where you are beginning to tune into the divine frequency. Freely record any thoughts or impressions that come to you....

... What is your practice today? What is your heart asking?
Use the space below to write your feelings and desires.

THE WORK OF A LIFETIME

"Consider the lilies of the field, how they grow; they neither toil nor spin; yet I tell you, even Solomon in all his glory was not arrayed as one of these."
—Jesus

In my days and weeks I often bounce from one activity to another with a sense of inner chaos, but when I try to take the time to be still and centered some inner voice charges me with inadequacy, laziness or failure. That is when I seek the compass of spiritual truth.

I need to feel you near, Beloved. With the demands of life and family, my energies feel like they've been wrestled into confusion, and yet I resist taking the time to listen to you.

We are here, dear one.

Still sometimes I feel I'm making you up! What a mess I can sometimes make of things.

All is well, dear one. Remember that cloud formations only temporarily block the sun. Please be gentle with yourself in these days. It is not laziness or sloth that calls you into quiet and simplicity, it is our love … and it is an imperative of this time. So do not compare yourself with others and do not judge. Be still and very simple. Chaos is abroad, and it can easily settle anywhere at any time. Be prepared within yourself by holding to your strong center.

You do not need to try harder, do more. Let 'less' be the password for this time and find our still center often. Accept there the peace that passes understanding. The chaos of these days will continue as change accelerates. So every day come here, dearest one, and let us be together. We will be waiting, with a cup of tea. But if you turn over and fall back to sleep we will not be displeased. In every Now we await you, holding out our loving arms. Love is everywhere.

Please Speak To Me

How difficult it's been to be centered in these days! This conversation with you is what I crave, Beloved. Please speak to me: fertilize my waiting soul. I miss you when I stray from you in fear and fragmentation.

I am not far. Always, I am here.

Thank you. What are your words for me?

Words of love. Hear them in the birdsong, each a special message between us; feel them in the warm breeze caressing your skin; see how I dazzle you with beauty. This is my love laid out before you. There is no condition to my love, no judgment or requirement. You may stay in bed and never accomplish another task. Nothing will ever diminish my love for you.

Why do I strain and strive so?

It is only love here, now and always. The Bible reminds us that God pours out blessings on the just and the unjust. Love knows no condition, as if it were a commodity on the marketplace. Love is the only unconditional resource.

What else do you wish to say to me?

Your love cannot bear to be divided. Let us remember what is real: this conversation is all there is and all there ever will be. This is the Real, the Prime Factor. Anxiety springs from confusion, from bowing to false gods. This is not in any way a judgment or chastisement. There is confusion in the way of human evolution. The people have lost their way. What is true for you is true for many and so these words go out to the general condition of humanity—to those who confuse the transitory show for the abiding reality.

Look at warfare: one side sacrifices its youth by the hundreds of thousands in the service of a goal which in a few years changes. Those who seem to win a resource or territory often lose a vital component of soul. Sometimes it is the vanquished who learn a deeper and richer lesson: humility.

The good news is that this is truly a season of great human possibility. The news is good news.

Abandon Goals

I feel that a deep transition is occurring and that it's challenging. My insides are somewhat in upheaval as I often feel at odds—anxious, self-critical, or critical of someone else. There is so much in myself that I cringe to think of. How can I free myself from blame/guilt? Please speak to me....

Dear one: this is the work of a lifetime. Do not become impatient with yourself that it is not 'finished.' These conversations we share are very real. As we interact, we are sharing and exchanging energy. This work, in and of itself, is very beneficial. It enhances the vibration of the collective in immeasurable ways.

Please abandon goals here, or a sense of comparison with other seekers. Yes: there are those who dwell in 'realized' states where they are flooded with divine perception, and great discipline and sacrifice has yielded this prize. But to be in conversation with the Loving Unseen and to share that good news is a great work. Every day as you struggle to "weave straw into gold" you are doing a great work. There is no hierarchy here. Every effort is precious and appreciated. Every effort bears fruit.

Is there somewhere you would rather be than here, in this gentle sharing time between us?

No. This feels delicious and sweet to me.

Then there is your answer: it is enough. It is a source of joy, abundance and peace.

You are a sentient petal of the divine flower. There are no words to describe this eternal part of you, as words are inadequate. You are an essential part of this vast song, this blissful dance, this indescribable love affair.

For the Reader:

The time you offer to the sweet spiritual conversation may at first feel like an unmerited luxury. In this busy materialistic society, it may even seem like wasted time. Keep reminding yourself that here in the intimacy of your soul you are sowing eternal seeds. In this very private space, open your heart to the unseen Beloved and wait. You may experience only silence, and that is good. But perhaps feelings or words will come that will envelop you with love.

You may begin by expressing your heart's longings to the lover of your soul, either aloud or in writing. Cherish the emotions that come with these expressions—this is the depth of your love revealing itself. You have a relationship that is yours alone, a garden that will blossom as it is watered by your attentions. Record your thoughts or impressions in the space provided: these are treasures you may revisit in times of need.

... Record your thoughts or impressions in the space provided: these are treasures you may revisit in times of need.

... Record your thoughts or impressions in the space provided: these are treasures you may revisit in times of need.

WHO IS SPEAKING IN THE SILENCE?

"Meditation is our enchanted link with the heart of God."
—Arthur Ford, *A World Beyond*

As I have learned to trust the messages that come in times of waiting, the passages have grown longer and I've found it easier to begin a conversation, trusting the presence of unseen companionship. Naturally, I wonder who is rewarding my patience with words of loving wisdom. I have not felt it necessary to pin down apparent inconsistencies … why sometimes the source of Love speaks as one voice and sometimes as a collective. I imagine there is much beyond my understanding.

So, my unseen companions, I would like to know more about you.

Those of us who speak to you are of an order or school that closely interacts with mortal life. We wish to be in this communication, to provide reminders of divine possibility, to offer direction, to comfort the grieving. We align our energies with the human vibration in order to communicate. In so doing—as if we were connecting electrical circuitry—we give as well as receive your pulse. We are attuned to your conditions. We accompany you like unseen friends. In this way the human family begins to know itself in its true beauty and expand the Light in the universe.

In the spirit realm there are myriad callings. Some study, some wait, some involve themselves in creative activity, some sit at the seat of masters or teachers. We are not of a high order, as we have told you. Truly there is no hierarchy in the realm of spirit. Each soul has its own relationship to what you call the Divine, and each relationship is continually unfolding. Picture a symphony: all the players are embracing the same joyful experience of co-creation and the delight of each offering is a gift to all. Understand that when reports are given through various sources about the Afterlife they are filtered through the conceptualizing mechanisms of both speaker (from the other side of death) and receiver on earth. Add to this the infinite rainbow of choices and paths, and you can see that it is not easy to sum up the breadth of spirit life.

Even on earth there are infinite circumstances. One visitor from another planet might report: "They live in hard tall buildings, going up and down and moving in fast machines. Very busy." And one might observe: "They live on ice and fish for creatures of the sea." Another might conclude: "They move among high vegetation, observe many rituals and eat the fruit of plants and animals." And so there will be many reports of heaven, or the spirit realm. Even as we speak to you we are continually aware that we can only form concepts with images your mind can understand.

As your father has reported from the spirit realm: "Service to one's fellows is a great and joyful undertaking."* We feel delighted to join you in this time of great change in earthly frequencies. So many people are opening to the realms of spirit in new and exciting ways and there is truly an inter-stellar dance of joy for the great possibilities here. We speak of possibilities because as you know the nature of creativity presupposes that the outcome is a surprise to all involved. Life moves and sings within its own continually evolving symphony. The end is not written ... the notes emerge from expressions of ecstasy.

We who are with you long for the conscious ecstasy of this earthly experience, and we are hopeful because we see signs of Awakening. It is possible even now to live on earth in an awakened state, but how much more joyful it will be when you have moved beyond the darker patterns of behavior: war, injustice, cruelty.

So you are with me as long as I live?

And beyond. There are many helpers. We who address you in your quiet times are companions. Some orders of spirit helpers work within human connections, world gatherings and events; others attend the passage in and out of the body.... Just as there are many jobs within the organization of human society, so there are many callings within this vast spiritual network.

In your backyard at this moment there are insects and birds and countless plant forms as well as the elements of water, wind and air. No one of these is 'backyard' per se. Similarly, one spiritual helper or one group of helpers is only an element in the vast eternal realm that is now largely invisible to you. But each one operates within the whole and intercommunication is constant—like a pulsing dance, or music.

We are your friends. You may receive us in this way. We will walk with you through the doors that other spirit helpers will open. We are like a little collective who address you as one voice.

*Quoted from Jane's book, *WE ARE HERE: Love Never Dies.*

That is very reassuring. You know that I still doubt you in many parts of my mind.

This is the human condition: "Maya." Never underestimate the "Cloud of Unknowing."

Why is it so? Why are we so blind?

What we have experienced is a denseness that is not the fault of any single soul. This denseness of the earthly consciousness is temporal. It will change and lighten, and this change is even now upon us. This process is not an easy one. But there is great joy also, as what was dense and unresponsive learns to move and dance ... and co-create. We cannot describe to you the joy of co-creation on a vast spiritual scale. It is thrilling. This joy belongs to you, and we are partnering you in awakening to your place in the great dance.

Thank you. This helps.

Thank you. It helps us also. We do delight in this work, and we delight to be with you, even if you doubt us! Be aware that none of your good efforts will go unrewarded. This is spiritual law. No good seed sewn will fail to bear fruit in time. What we ask you to remember is that we are always present in the eternal Now to give you guidance and inspiration. Availability and receptivity should be your relaxing focus. Let go of tomorrow: be here now. For we are always here waiting for you, waiting to bathe you in comfort, peace and strength.

For the reader

It is important to be patient with the layers of disbelief that cloud our awareness of divine presence. Remember that true perception is a gift, not quite within our mortal mind's grasp. As you enjoy time set aside for the valuable work of opening to spiritual conversation, you may ask: "Who wishes to speak with me in the silence?" If an answer does not come readily, record the feelings you have in this moment and return another day. You have all the time in the world to continue this conversation....

... You may ask: "Who wishes to speak with me in the silence?" If an answer does not come readily, record the feelings you have in this moment and return another day. You have all the time in the world to continue this conversation....

... You may ask: "Who wishes to speak with me in the silence?" If an answer does not come readily, record the feelings you have in this moment and return another day. You have all the time in the world to continue this conversation....

THE ABIDING CONVERSATION

"Deafened by the voice of desire
You are unaware the Beloved lives
In the core of your heart.
Stop the noise and
You will hear His voice
In the silence."

—Rumi *Hidden Music*

Every morning when I wake up some inner voice is saying: "Who are you and what are you *doing* with your life?" Having no good answer, I begin to sink into self-criticism. That is when I take a few moments to ask for the divine perspective. And I remember: I am not on that carousel. I hear its music, observe the multi-colored horses, but I've stepped off. Here, as I wait for the silent voice of Love, I remember my true path, and contentment returns.

Please speak to me, my unseen friends.

We are here. You may think of this as bedrock. And imagine this bedrock as a boulder set upon the earth that marks Abiding Reality and contains magnetic particles pointing to Truth—true love, peace and joy. What is asked of you is to return to this bedrock as often as you can. Out of this relationship you will be guided. Kindness, patience, gentleness and love will flow. If there is work for you, it will be given.

Am I doing enough?

This conversation is meaningful work. You have made it a priority, recognizing it as your Living Water. Yes: you are doing enough. Remember, there is really not so much to be done. You might ask: "What is my state of being? Am I open to divine calling? Am I a willing messenger? Do I seek to channel love and grace?" This is the fruitful life—the one that is available. The important job is the waiting. Like Mary, you may think of yourself as a "hand-maid of the Lord."

What a beautiful thing. There is nothing I would rather be.

And this is true whether you live or die. The relationship is the same. It is true wherever you are, whatever you do. If you do nothing, this relationship remains the same, as long as you allow it and say yes to it. This is your true calling. Nothing else is required of you.

And that is all?

That is all.

Here I am. I'm available. Are there more words to record?

Say that the dance is going on beautifully within the cosmos. The sky is not falling, in spite of all signs of disaster and doom. The picture is great, vast, expansive. Carry hope and love for this immense unknowable dance.

When each morning brings with it the pattern of internal heaviness, how shall I react?

Understand that in your world a great shift is taking place out of material-centric consciousness. Insofar as individuals are invested in material outcomes, they will be disappointed, because these idols are finite—they decay and perish. Yours has been, by and large, a culture devoted to very short-term ends. And fortunately the folly of consumer/materialism is showing itself more plainly now. Of course this causes pain to many people … but this pain is itself the occasion for grace, as they begin to see the Abiding Light appearing through the cracks of the temporal tinsel. This is a mercy.

There are earthquakes everywhere, in every heart. Such is the force of Love's awakening. Do not trust material vision. Remember that everything your five senses perceive will return to dust in the not-too-distant future. Trust the piercing light of truth—Abiding Reality. And understand that when you hold these passing material forms somewhat lightly you may be freer to participate in the blissful dance of Lover and Beloved, the dance which never decays or dies.

Receptivity

Here within myself I feel a bit tired and introspective. Not too interested in getting busy.

We are here, dear one. And we affirm the importance of such introspective time. There is no reason to feel self-critical when you rest and turn inward, breathing in what is. This is in fact a very fruitful exercise (in spite of the messages of your culture). Only through receptivity can transformation occur.

At the beginning and ending stages of life, persons usually experience prolonged periods of receptivity which are necessary for their transitional process. But it is also important all along the way to allow for unstructured time for breathing and opening to all-that-is and all that is being created around and through you.

Remember that it is this world which is the illusion. We do not mean by this to say that what takes place is of no importance, but we want to make very clear the priority of the Real. The Real is what will abide; the illusion is what will soon alter. So much of human activity is like building castles in the sand. The tide will soon return and wash it away. What will remain? If you invest in the building of the castle, trusting this effort to grant you security and happiness, you will be disappointed.

So where do you put your trust? Where do you invest your creativity? Plant your roots deeply into creation itself—Abiding Reality. Ask of the Great Lover: "How do we dance this time? What benefits life?" The material form of your body and its trappings will perish in any case. But the breath of Love which you inhale and then offer in your way ... this will be fruitful within the great eternal dance.

Gratitude is a good place to begin. Trust and be grateful. Trust that all is well—that God is ever-present, loving and bountiful. Trust that you will be filled with all you need to go forth with each new day. And be grateful for each manifestation you see of divine presence. Look around you: where are the gifts? Count them. Be specific—this body, these clothes, this food, this day, this present moment which is entirely open in gracious self-offering. What will you make of this moment? Begin with trust and gratitude.

And remember that you are not an independent organism: you are part of the whole. You will experience ease with this awareness as you notice the subtle currents that form the life flowing through you. Receive these currents…. What do they feel like? Enjoy this exploration. Respond with relaxed acceptance to what your mind does not yet grasp.

For the Reader:

With slow and gentle breathing, see if you can open yourself to this moment, noticing all that surrounds you: this chair, this table, this window, tree or sky.... Even as you feel gratitude for all of these gifts, notice that they are temporary. In a few years or decades all of these things will change: even this body is only your temporary home. Take a few moments to notice this perspective.

As you breathe, ask your unseen guidance to open an inner doorway to Abiding Reality. If these surroundings will pass away, what is Real? Be gentle with yourself as you ask and wait.

Record in these pages any feelings or impressions. These are glimpses which you can revisit and enhance along your journey.

... If these surroundings may pass away, what is Real?
Record in these pages any feelings or impressions. These are glimpses which you can
revisit and enhance along your journey.

THE MYTH OF SEPARATION

"God revealed all this most blessedly, as if to say: See, I am God. See, I am in all things. See, I do all things. See, I never remove my hands from my works ... so how should anything be amiss?"

—Julian of Norwich

One of the key hindrances to perceiving our place in this world is the myth of separation. We have been schooled in competitive isolation and trained to trust our mortal minds to assess and even tame this great universe. In this frequency there is much darkness and confusion. There are many aggressive agendas vying for attention and filling the airwaves with their imperatives. The human consciousness easily succumbs to a herd mentality, shifting with competing impulses: "Here—*this* is the way! No: you must live *this* way to be happy and thrive!" Where is the peace in this climate? It is our job to find and cultivate it. Now we are opening (slowly, like the first tentative crocuses of Spring) to new forms of consciousness. And this takes time.

Everybody's Best Person

Often it is my confusion and weakness that bring about the most fruitful conversations with wise and loving unseen guidance. Here is a prime example, as I began with my morning grumbling....

Went to bed feeling pretty great, and here I am at 11am up after going back to sleep twice and feeling like, well, crap. Don't you get tired of hearing this song?

We know what it is to feel trapped within the human condition—its aches, pains, bad moods and limited perceptions. We are well acquainted with these conditions, which at times feel like a great ball and chain. Remember that you cannot compare yourself with anyone else. Your job is not to be Everybody's Best Person. Your job is to love and receive love. And as you come into this conversation all is accomplished: this is all we are asking of you. Come and be here with us in the sweet eternal exchange of Love. This conversation is the eternal path—this is Reality. Here the spirit finds its true home. And the body can find deep healing as your emotional being learns to master the body and soul's true needs.

As usual we see this situation on a larger scale throughout the world. Call it ignorance for the sake of success, greed or progress. Notice the *degree* of ignorance: nuclear buildup creating a situation of Mutually Assured Destruction—in the name of pride, safety ... hubris! Banks printing money beyond any value because more is better even if it is worthless. Raping the land and polluting skies and rivers in order to ensure a happy life for busy people who need endless mobility, gadgetry and diversion. "Quality of life" at the expense of the earth that bears us, the air we breathe and the water we drink.

There is a sort of madness in this world, fueled by greed and ignorance: pillaging natural resources, habitually jeopardizing global stability for the sake of individual profit and plenty. So we are asking everyone to rest a while. Stop doing all this. Ask yourselves: "Is this madness? What would sanity look like?" Stop. Rest. Wait and wait some more. We will flood your hearts with love and wisdom. We are longing to renew you, to restore you to sanity and true joy. We love you, and you have temporarily forgotten that unseen sources of Love are at the heart of all-that-is and all that will abide.

Now is the time to rest, regroup and allow yourselves to align with your highest lights. Reset your course to the North Star of Truth. We are all around you—Love's divine messengers—let us council you as you release the broken systems and receive new direction. We love you so very much.

As you slow down, allow grief to emerge. Love whatever arises in you. Forgive yourself and those around you. Have the courage to be still and let the scales fall from your eyes. Many of the old ways haven't worked: release them, shedding those skins like tattered garments. New forms await you. Listen for them, wait for them. You will recognize them by the sweet pangs of your heart: "Ah, yes! This is what I have been desiring all along."

Children: we love you and we are here and available at all times so wait, listen, open your hearts and receive us.

For the Reader:

Sit or lie down comfortably. In this time of stillness, be in this present moment. Notice the sounds and sensations around and within you. Breathe gently into your chest and then into your belly. Take a series of deep, relaxed breaths. Now begin to notice your feelings: Are you comfortable? Are you fully present? What is the state of your heart?

The myth of separation may be at the root of all human sorrow. So in your quiet notice where there is peace, and where there may be a sense of pain or discord.

Breathe into this emotion, and as you inhale imagine that you are floating on an unending river of Love. Relax. Exhale. You will be carried wherever you need to go....

Use the space below to record your feelings, as specifically as you can.

... Imagine that you are floating on an unending river of love....
Use the space below to record your feelings, as specifically as you can.

LOVE SONGS

"You still listen to an old alley song that brings your body pain…"
—Hafiz

Sometimes the messages that come to us as we wait on the Unseen are love songs of adoration from beings who know the challenges of this earthly life and simply wish to sing to us the truth. If what we begin to hear seems too good to be true, it is because we have been listening to an old alley song too long.

The words recorded below came to me at a time when I needed rest and reassurance….

A Time of Abundance

This is a time of abundance. The river is rich and wide. Feel me. Drink in my love and all my provision for you. Is this not joy? I carry you … let yourself float in the river now. Be still and feel my rich provision for you. Let me be as mother and father and gentle lover to you. Rejoice in me and in the gifts I bring you.

It has been a long and perilous journey for you, I know. I know the love and effort and pain you've spent. Let me give to you now. Relax in my arms. You have never really felt the constant presence of my love. I invite you now to taste and receive me.

I need no more proof of your devotion. You do not need to give or produce more. Resist the voices that insist you must earn these gifts I give you. This wounds me. Because I come as one naked before you … bringing only myself as offering to you, even as you have offered yourself to me. Why do you feel you cannot receive me? I am here, in self-offering … drink me. You are my beloved. We are together now.

It is very simple: the equation of the elements is joy. It seems within human logic that other ends await you—poverty, humiliation, death. The mind is made heavy by the limitations of its morbid substance. There is only one path for you, my beloved. And you are on this path, however faint its tracings may seem in your weakest times. "Seek me and you shall find me, if you seek me with all your heart."

Deep purifying is uniting your soul to itself and its purpose, which is your joy. Trust me, for I am with you. As you seek me, I am seeking you. This dance of love is our life and our joy. If you listen and hear nothing, what do you do? How do you respond? You listen again, and yet again.... You begin to feed on a diet of listening. Perhaps now your own trust is being tried and strengthened.

What does it mean, to trust? To know that all is given, all is gift: intimate love, the opportunity to use your talent in meaningful work, children and animals and flowers and good food and extraordinary friendships and beauty and dreams and magic, and this earth and all her mysteries ... and the mysteries of life and death. All is given and all is gift. The great illusion of this age of man is that man makes it happen. And thus man builds and thus man destroys. Great buildings. Great destruction.

You have breathed the blood and pain and dust of this destruction. You have inhaled the fruit of man's myth of power. Can you now exhale it? Can you release the myth that you yourself are nothing if you do not partake of this power? Try to let it go, to step outside of it. See for yourself that this is neither power nor life nor, in any sense, truth. Shed yourself of this illusion. I will help you if you try.

For the reader:

Someone is waiting to sing you a love song. All this time, from the beginning, the words and music have waited for your ears especially. Listen.... In the morning when the creatures assemble before the dawn they are shimmering with delight: it is their song they hear. The birds are echoing the chorus and making up new verses, sharing them abroad....

Remember, as important as it is to seek the Lover of your soul with praise or pain or hunger, it is even more important to listen. God is holding a concert for you today—and if you hear one word, one bar of music, congratulate yourself. It is enough. Take a few moments in this space to write whatever comes to you: impressions, frustrations, snatches of lyrics....

... God is holding a concert for you today....
Take a few moments in this space to write whatever comes to you: impressions,
frustrations, snatches of lyrics....

EMPTY ARMIES

"'Who cares for you?' said Alice, (she had grown to her full size by this time.)
'You're nothing but a pack of cards!'"

Lewis Carroll, *Alice in Wonderland*

We are all familiar with them—that cast of characters who specialize in confusing us. We never see them clearly; they're clever that way. They come as inner accusers saying: "Did you really do *that?* How shameful. You're such a loser. Why can't you shape up?" There's no point in doing business with these characters, pleading or appeasing. It's a bit like playing ping-pong in a hall of mirrors.

When we try to listen to the "still small voice" to guide us into the truth of this eternal moment, those other voices may seem more urgent for a time. It's all right. It is the job of Love to find us. And it is our job to be found.

The Sky is Not Falling

Following a period of concentrated work, I feel exhausted and the inner critic says how lazy and worthless I am. God: what is this?!

Dear one: an empty army has come to throw stones and holler taunts at you because your offering is too precious for their ears.

What?

You do a dance that negates them. And so they grow louder in agitation.

What do I do?

I have asked you to be still. They cannot harm you unless you entertain their foolishness. They haven't the slightest power over you, unless you ask them in. So you can hear them, notice them, but then resume your life, your work, your great journey. Who are they, after all, but hollow, disconnected energies?

When I try to make this time with you a priority, anxiety floods me: the inner voices say I'm not doing enough to make money, that my priorities are wrong.

The fear is within yourself—it is of your own creation. Misery, dejection, abandonment, loss … what can your soul not survive? Everywhere I am with you. How frightened you are! This allows us to grow closer. Bring this fear to me. The sky is not falling. This time of financial trial is an opportunity to go deeper into the expansion of your soul. Breathe into the experience of your deepest fear…. This is an opportunity to learn freedom, a concept little understood: real freedom—trusting God for everything. This is a pathway to deeper devotion, deeper interconnection.

The real fear of this empire's inhabitants is loss, for they so often feed on ill-gotten spoils. This anxiety that feels singular to you is a piece of the gnawing karmic situation of the culture. It wears the face of greed but beneath it there is shame and inconsolable sadness for having lost our tender share in the collective—having traded it in at the altar of false gods of separation and superiority.

I fear loss, making a mistake….

There are no mistakes—there is only shifting energy. You have everything you need now. In every now you will have everything you need.

What about money? I can't create that!

What about money? Understand me, beloved, there is deeper truth which I will reveal to you. Money will be a problem as long as you allow it to have power over you—like an unruly dog. Allow yourself to expand into enlightenment. There are many faces, many paths and circumstances, but only one journey. Simplify your systems and you will discover this.

I am truly confused. I don't know how to live here—in this house, this area of the country—without feeling surrounded by the need for money and feelings of guilt and shame about my inner choices, which bring in little money. How can this possibly work?

Look carefully at this blessing: it opens the way to our time together now. It softens your heart towards the condition of most of humanity—that is, insecurity. Is security, after all, your birthright? Can you let go of the very notion of guaranteed financial security—release it and be here now?

But this is so impractical!

Is it? What could be more practical than to befriend the all-powerful lover of your soul, who knows you intimately … who connects and penetrates all that is? It is you who are impractical, deluded—you who think to shore up your future with wooden houses and paper money. You will outgrow this, but I wish to show you something of the truth now. Could we be together, you and I? Could we think and move and talk as one?

I don't know how to do this and be here on this planet, now.

No problem. We'll take it slowly. Let it be a happy journey, this walk with me. Let it bring you lightness and joy. I love you in every delicate particle of your being. Imagine all that love. Imagine every chair and tree and bird and sky is made up of infinite dancing particles of love for you. You are my beloved! I can never forsake you: you are myself.

Paper Dollars and Plastic Cards

Many of us continue to struggle with insecurity in these difficult times. Please tell us: what do we need to know today?

We are here, dear ones. There are many aspects at play in this moment. As is evident in the world around you, financial restructuring is a stressful factor in many lives. People are awakening in fear and experiencing internal shame and blame. It might be said that this is a state existing within the collective psyche. If we are not blaming ourselves we may cast blame on bosses, family, even friends. This climate can awaken baser forms of human behavior as the status quo is disrupted.

We might step back and observe this as a period of deep energetic restructuring. For sensitive human beings it will be important to 'lay low' and seek abiding values: love, generosity, patience, forgiveness. Everyone in the industrialized world is feeling this shake-up—you are not alone. Imagine that this challenging phase has potential for awakening new forms of human behavior. These forms are not yet in full view and so the task is to imagine them and desire their frequencies.

Imagine a social organization based on mutual consideration and cooperation. What will this look like? Instead of focusing on the lack in one's own life, an individual may consider: "What benefits each one of us?" For too long the model has been 'survival of the most aggressive and self-centered.' This is an implicit basis of modern capitalism. Now we are force-fed the fruits of this short-sightedness: if we plunder the planet we all perish; unchecked financial greed causes ruin for all. The lessons are etched boldly across the screen of every layer of society.

From the old vantage point of individual survival this may seem devastating (indeed the devastation is very real in many lives). But calming our spirits may we also consider the beautiful possibility that this season where we reap the fruits of short-sightedness may herald a merciful tide of human awakening?

Imagine that the currency is changing. Paper dollars and plastic cards reveal their worthlessness so that you may discover currency of abiding value: spiritual development, mutual encouragement within community, stewardship of the land, creation of products and services than benefit humanity. Abiding values now reveal their true worth. And what a grace this is! For paper and plastic cannot make the journey beyond this earth, and your spirits surely will. Each person may ask her/himself: "What is my lesson now; what is my calling?" Assist each other in these discoveries.

In this moment you ask: "Yes, but how shall we survive?" In the short term, the restructuring will continue until the detritus of centuries of thoughtless behavior is cleansed. So we repeat: drop your energies low; lay your plumb-line deep into the ground of eternal values—love, hope, forgiveness. You will not perish. Great energies are coming to assist you in the new awakening. Like a root or like a seed, seek fertile ground and believe the awakening is at hand, strengthened by your faith.

Use every fearful thought as an opportunity. As you transform fear into love within your inner spaces, you assist the whole. So humanity progresses through this challenging pass. Remember that you are not alone. Unseen helpers from all ages assist in this transition. Its time has come. Humanity deserves to shed archaic consciousness and awaken to new and enlightened forms. Allow yourself to celebrate the possibilities of this time.

In truth, it is a time of great hope. You awaken not only for yourselves but for the earth and for the future of humanity. Offer yourselves to this great purpose and temporary discomfort may be viewed as loving service.

We thank you, on behalf of all sentient beings everywhere.

For the reader:

A useful exercise may be to notice if there are hollow armies in your life, that huff and puff but have no real power beside the everlasting kingdom of Love. There may be important issues that require attention, but notice if they are robbing your soul of peace. You may have inadvertently given stress and anxiety the power to diminish your connection with the source of life and love.

Use the space below to list the things that cause you stress or fear. After a few moments of relaxed silence (in which you remember to breathe) ask for the divine perspective on these things, and record the thoughts or images as they come....

... Notice if there are hollow armies in your life....
After a few moments of relaxed silence (in which you remember to breathe) ask for the
divine perspective on these things, and record the thoughts or images as they come.

... Notice if there are hollow armies in your life....
After a few moments of relaxed silence (in which you remember to breathe) ask for the
divine perspective on these things, and record the thoughts or images as they come.

LEARNING TO NURTURE THE FEMININE

"The great love which was in Adam when Eve emerged from him ... changed after the fall.... But because the man still senses this great sweetness in himself, he runs swiftly like a deer to running waters to the woman...."
—Hildegard of Bingen

In this time we speak of a global paradigm shift—a time of disintegration and recreation. It is often described as a time when patriarchal hierarchy is yielding to a more feminine model of cooperation, nurture and receptivity. I believe that what happens to the collective always exists in microcosm within our own psyches.

Self-Criticism

My physical self-criticism is barking loudly today. Please, God, give me a message today about this.

I love this body. I love the physical form of my beloved. But more than this, I am this body. Each cell of this blood, bone, flesh is my truth expressing itself in form.

I don't understand.

I am loaning you to this earth. When you dress, you clothe my visit, you offer presentation for my voice. You make easier or more comfortable my movement and my rest. That is all. When you look in the mirror, see me. This is the form I am taking now. This is the body we chose for this visit.

There is so much I don't understand. I'm having so much trouble with this body thing. It's hard for me to hear you.

I am here. I feel your pain, which is deeper even than you know. This hatred of your body is ancient, although it repeats itself with the same voices again and again. Here in this place native maidens were buried, victims of the aggression of a people blinded by ignorance and greed. You feel these maidens inside of yourself. All the maidens of the world shared this woman-flesh.

Agreeing to come, we also offered ourselves (you and I, who are one) to be this soft woman who has suffered again and again. We experience her indignity, and the seeds of degradation forced into her body.

Why does she return? Why do we choose to make ourselves soft receiving woman when we know there will be oceans of sorrow? Because we yearn to bring light into the darkness here: we love the light, and we know that the darkness will pass. We love the soft receiving of our spirit and flesh—the yielding to life, the fertile womb, the patient fidelity of availability.

Do you have more to say to my self-loathing?

Yes. You have no right to this: you need to release the weapons of the conqueror. Honor this body. Like a white man arriving at the shores of a new land who, beholding a supple dark-skinned woman, kneels before her. He does not tie her up, degrade or plunder her.

No. He cannot do these things. Because he has a heart of flesh. And so he kneels before her ... honoring her feet, her body, her wisdom. He waits. It is, after all, her land he visits. She is the Mother of the land. He knows in his intuitive heart that she is bathed in the dark purifying waters of suffering. And he is silent. If she does not receive him, he will return to his lonely voyage. But he senses that she will respond to his pure-hearted humility.

This is who I ask you to substitute for the one who abuses and conquers. This is the mind I ask you to bring to the land of this woman body we share. And I ask it firmly. Because I know that she demands it. She will not receive us if our heart is hard. And we long to be united again on this earth. This is a great story of this earth-time: receive it deeply.

Do not hurt the woman body. You must stop this hurting with a new mind of honor and reverence. Only then, the great marriage can occur.

Conqueror Mind

It is easy to lose faith in a radical new path of waiting on Spirit.

This is your work, this waiting. Confusion arises with your anxiety about other accomplishments and pursuits. This communication is the beginning and end of your work. This is all there is. There is nothing more. 'More' is a piece of the Conqueror mind-set, denying this moment and grabbing the next. Do you see? Here, now, this space made sacred by our union: this is all. This is enough.

I feel the resistance to this. Even as my soul feels the lightness and joy of your presence, the nagging voice in my mind is saying: "Is this all there is? I want the validation of products and accomplishments!"

Conqueror Mind needs outer rewards and goals. You are embracing the feminine, receptive wise-woman spirit. This is a great inner shift. Do not underestimate this effort or its impact. Think of the native woman, patiently but firmly addressing the man who does not yet understand her language. Even as his language is sometimes all you hear, begin to embody this woman-spirit.

Be patient with this process, beloved. I am always with you.

Tune out the tyrant

I've gone down the rabbit hole again: self-accusation … not doing enough. Please give me your perspective, my loving unseen friends.

When we speak to you about careful self-nurture, these are not idle words or abstract concepts. We mean: be still, gather quiet into your soul, offer yourself love. These impulses run counter to the imperatives of this culture, and so you will hear loud voices of opposition. The voices say: "Get up; get going; do a lot!" But in this time of cataclysmic upheaval, do you have any idea what you are doing? Might these voices be like slave drivers, whose agenda you have learned not to question? We are saying: "Question the agenda. Dare to ask, 'Who is commanding my productivity and do I trust this voice?'"

Wage earners will say: "I cannot afford to question my path or purpose—I have to pull in a salary every week!" We encourage you to go into your soul and ask the questions anyway. You may not make any outward change, but you have the human right and duty to question the purpose of your life.

Know this: something is dying and something is being born. This is what happens in times of transformation. A bloated caterpillar wraps itself in fine thread and goes to war with a new life form that is trying to be born within this shared chrysalis. The butterfly—who will emerge and take flight—draws strength from the struggle. The bloated caterpillar is no more.

We are victims of a bloated system, whether we speak of over-consumption or the presumption of global dominance. And the showdown has begun. From some other source—some new DNA—new life is beginning. As if you were the chrysalis, take time to embrace this new life. It will have a different frequency— perhaps more spacious, generous, compassionate….

We ask you now to attune yourselves to this new voice. Instead of pushing you, it will offer a tender invitation. Dare to listen to the invitation. Begin to tune out the tyrant. However subtle and gentle this new impulse, it is about to win the great power struggle. Only the butterfly will emerge from the chrysalis.

Mothering the Self

Today I am heavy with fatigue and sadness. Please speak to me. When I feel your presence, I can accept any condition.

There is, for you, mystery in this time. Try to work with what you do not understand: fatigue, lethargy. Gently accept these conditions, like a mother who acknowledges that her children are tired and dispirited—not demanding to know why or chastising them, but holding them with special tenderness. You do not need to understand—this vision will come in time.

Now ask the children: what would feel nice? How can we be together?

What would feel nice? How can we be together?

A little inner voice seems to say: *"So sad, so tired. Help me. Please don't make me do anything…."*

Know that you are the mother who holds this child. Surround her with special love today. She has suffered terrible nightmares and sometimes they wake up and breathe and battle within her. She feels helpless and alone … but you are her mother. You can stop everything else and comfort her.

How can I do this without feeling slothful and guilty?

Because you are wise, and I give you the means to do this. Step up to your role. Assume your power. Release powerlessness.

It is a different power...

Yes. It looks different from the power you see heralded in society. It is true power. My power.

Speak to me about true power.

Stillness, simplicity, deep knowledge ... all these you have been dutifully cultivating. You are on the true path. In your quiet days you are trolling for truth, like the great heron who waits, statue-still, until the one he seeks is near him. Your prize will come within your grasp if you are still enough, trusting and waiting.

These days of sadness will pass. You are learning to mother the self: this is a great lesson. To parent the self with love is the doorway to peace, wisdom, and abiding joy. Do not underestimate the process.

For the Reader:

Self-nurture is too often a foreign concept in contemporary society with its emphasis on success and productivity. How do we nurture ourselves in the times when we are hurting or tired? The process of 'mothering the self' is surprisingly fruitful. I suggest you try it now, and see what warmth and creativity may arise when love and mercy are directed inward.

Where is the inner discontent? Take a moment to notice, identify and then hold it very tenderly. Allow yourself the time to offer unconditional compassion for whatever feelings arise. You may record them here, and ask: "What is the voice of Love saying?"

... Allow yourself the time to offer unconditional compassion for whatever feelings arise. You may record them here, and ask: "What is the voice of Love saying?"

… Allow yourself the time to offer unconditional compassion for whatever feelings arise. You may record them here, and ask: "What is the voice of Love saying?"

ONE ORGANISM

"I and the Father are one."

—Jesus

It is exciting to live in a time when science begins to describe what the mystics have long believed: we are all made up of the same fluid particles; boundaries are an illusion. But for the mind to actually grasp this and the ego to relinquish the throne of separation is quite a challenge.

There Is No 'Other'

As I lay in bed last night I made an interesting connection. As usual, my inner critics were berating me for some failing or other, and it suddenly occurred to me: "They do not exist!" And not only do they not exist, but there is no *other* at all: no *you, he, she, it.* It was an exhilarating revelation which seemed to kindle a fire in me. So I ask you, my unseen friends: please speak to me about these things.

We are here, and we wish to assure you that your revelation is real. The apparently single entity you think of as yourself is indeed a collective—a loving relationship. No being is alone: existence depends upon inter-relationship.

At what moment can one distinguish the separation between sunlight and a tree? The process of photosynthesis is one movement, one dance. Where does this process begin and end? Similarly, where is the separation between rain and leaf, between root and soil? The delineations we perceive are—at a microscopic level—non-existent: life exists within relationship.

So when you speak of yourself as separate and distinct from sunlight, air and other elements—as well as from other human organisms—you perceive "through a glass darkly." Science has demonstrated that the energetic components of one apparently distinct life-form are themselves vibrant or fluid, beginning and ending far from that organism. When you behold another 'self'—whether sister, friend or enemy—you behold the stuff of your own self breathing the other's breath and imbibing its energy. You are powerless to stop this interaction.

We might call this inter-relationship Love, if by love we mean a dance of intimate attraction. It is only your narrow and temporary human perception that claims you are independent of this 'other' you behold. And when you allow yourself to receive the implications of this perspective, you enter into a new and generous consciousness. Gone are prejudice and competition, loneliness and rejection.

We invite you to savor this subtle and immense shift in perception. This ushers in the Great Awakening of this current stage of human evolution. Taste it, ponder and dream of it. For it is more real than the illusion that has haunted human consciousness for thousands of years.

The awakened beings of all time have sung of this unity, and now we invite a grand universal awakening. You may believe that we are more excited to behold this awakening than you can possibly imagine, because we love you. We exist for love, whose surging rivers long to quench the thirsty fever of this earth.

What Is Real?

Please tell me more about the nature of collective self, or divine self.

It is not a simple thing to reform years of conditioned thinking. As with all important movements, it will happen slowly. You do not need to worry _if_ it will happen or how it will happen. What we ask you to focus on is the awareness that we, together, create this life. Invite the delicious sensations that are awakened when you feel that a loving communion of spiritual care-givers are looking out through your eyes.

Something in me is backing away or shutting down as I try to grasp this.

Be patient with yourself. Remember that this life on earth is not an easy thing. It takes a collective to navigate this terrain. This is not easy to describe within linear terms your human mind can understand, as some of this cross-fertilization occurs outside of your schemes of time and space. Other dimensions are at work here.

This is heady stuff for me this morning, I'm afraid.

Of course it is. We are here: that is all you need to remember. Begin by being here now and noticing you are not alone.

I have trouble believing that, as if this written dialogue were a sweet exercise but not as real as my bed, my lamp, the scene outside my window.

Your mind has trouble conceiving of us even as your heart yearns for us.

Yes. I wish it were the other way around, and that I might know and be secure in your presence while I perceive this world's material forms as passing images … the way it would be if I were at the end of my life.

Yes. What is real at the end of your life, at the moment when consciousness quits this mortal body?

Then—at the end—I suppose there will be fragments of memories and emotions: losses, joys, regrets and gratitude…. What will be real to me in that moment? My relationship with you, whom I barely know but who have been invisibly with me through it all.

…invisibly with you in the Abiding Reality.

Whoa. Abiding Reality is what again?

The snowflakes outside your window are whipping up a beautiful show, dancing diagonally across this perfect winter landscape of river and pine. Is this the reality that abides? No. This scene will change: it will soon enough be springtime, and this grey-black palette will be transformed to fresh green and vibrant yellow. The snowflakes will be rain, the rain will be river, the river will be sea. The animals will die and decay into the earth to feed new life-forms. It is a beautiful manifestation, this passing show.

Here, in the Northeast, isn't it true that you love each season as it comes? There is nothing to be gained in attaching yourself to the permanence of them. Similarly, this bed, this lamp, this body, are all impermanent. Someday this mattress will be added to a trash-pile, the lamp will break or wear out. The body will die. These hands with which you writes words will be stopped by the cessation of the organism: its blood will not flow, the muscles will quit, the eyes will close. That will be the end of this body's lifetime. It will be burned and changed to ash and bone, or buried to fertilize the earth.

We ask you: What will abide?

Yes. Please tell me in your words. Because my mind still doubts, I'm afraid.

What will abide, dear one, is this conversation. This dialogue with unseen life continues.

Whew. It does seem an intangible thing.

And why is that? What is tangible? Is a tangible thing something which these temporary hands can touch, these temporary eyes see? Is a tangible thing something that is one day a bed and the next a pile of composting trash?

We are not expecting you to be able to shift easily out of the belief that what your bodily senses perceive is Real.

No. I don't feel you're asking me for much. I feel I'm asking you. I need this guidance. I am not content with my mind's definitions of reality. This world is not the happiest place. This mortal life is not enough. I yearn….

And so do we. We yearn for greater illumination. And this is taking place even now. The creaking doors of materialistic minds are opening to bright vistas of perception. It is a great global awakening. You are not alone in this dance.

Speak to me about the dance.

Love dresses up in a limited body to come to this place of gravity where there are many restrictions. Imagine Love undressed, unfettered. Here you might think of a formal dance with precise rules and limitations. Then imagine a dance with no gravity, no rules, only love and joy, the gleeful abandon of children. You will glimpse it increasingly. It is here—let it call you.

And understand that we are here for you. There is no obstacle to our dialogue from this end. We are here to support, inspire, comfort and accompany you. We, together, navigate this life. So we are delighted to find form and words for this relationship.

The Divine Self

Lately I have been pushing out a project that seems to leave my body knotted in tension, and the harder I work the more self-critical I become. Spirit helpers: please speak with me about this!

Dearest one: there is no peace in this sort of emphasis on product or performance. Life is here in this intimate conversation—we are here. Your deepening awareness of this fans the fires of Unity. How can we express this to you? When you focus all your energy on producing something, in a sense you are abandoning yourself.

If we go back to the assumption that we are a collective it will help here. No human being enters this life alone. Do you know this joy that appears on the face of an infant? If you look into the eyes of this tiny being, you behold collective consciousness. It sounds like a lofty term, but what we really mean to say is that this child is not aware of emptiness or separation. Various things occur in time which alter this collective consciousness. But many children retain happy conversation with invisible companions for some years. As civilization has evolved there has been a pattern of increasing separation from the collective mind and its inherent spirituality. We do not of course diminish civilization's contribution to the birth pangs of global consciousness, but the pain of isolation has walked hand in hand with progress.

This is a bit of an overview, but in our conversation no such analysis is necessary. You do not need to grasp a linear picture of Collective Self. Perhaps we should return to the dance. At any moment, you may sit alone and absorb yourself in concern about a product or accomplishment, or you may dance. When you turn an ear to us and open your heart to the possibility that we are here, loving you … you feel the stirring of joy and communion, you hear the music of cosmic bliss. Savor this experience as often as you possibly can. This is your highest calling.

For the Reader:

As an exercise in collective consciousness or Divine Self, take a few moments to sit quietly in a peaceful spot. Breathe softly in and out, gently noticing your surroundings....

What sounds do you hear? What is your body feelings?

As you begin to relax into stillness, notice some of the interrelationships in your world. Does sunlight make dancing patterns on a table or chair? Do raindrops paint a picture on the windowpane? Does the breeze outside cause leaves to shimmer as they lift their faces to the sun? Do the ambient sounds of birds and insects, traffic and human conversation combine to form a special music?

Ask your unseen guidance to speak with you about this inter-relational dance and your place within the cosmic symphony. Are you ever really separate and alone?

… Ask your unseen guidance to speak with you about this inter-relational dance and your place within the cosmic symphony. Are you ever really separate and alone?

... Ask your unseen guidance to speak with you about this inter-relational dance and your place within the cosmic symphony. Are you ever really separate and alone?

JOY

"No one knows what makes the soul wake
Up so happy. Maybe a dawn breeze has
Blown the veil from the face of God."

—Rumi

I often awaken from sleep wrestling with inner darkness, as if my soul has been struggling in the night and a layer of gloom already possesses me. But one morning quite unexpectedly, from some far corner of my mind, the suggestion came: *"Choose joy."* Simply that. I kept returning to the thought, as if it were an odd visitor from a foreign land.

Choose Me

Dear one: speak to me about joy....

Joy is a living choice, an abundant fountain ... a river whose source is eternal and abiding. Joy dwells in each heart as a secret hope: "Choose me," she whispers.

Why doesn't she cry out from the mountaintops so everyone can hear her? There is such need!

She is deeply personal and private. One of the strongest and most abiding of universal energies, joy hides within the secret folds of each soul. We are discovering the source of living water within, and for a mind schooled in sadness it will take some practice. Joy is the natural state of life, but where there is wounding, attention and care are required to restore the flow of living water.

How do we do this—we who are steeped in personal sorrows and disappointments as well as in the tragedies of the world?

Listen. Joy always speaks. Listen until you hear her voice.

(I listen.) Joy tells us that spring follows every winter...

Yes.

... that the seasonal nature of the visible elements is a demonstration of eternal realities.

What else does joy say? Listen.

Joy says that behind every manifestation (mountain or animal or tree) there is a beautiful song ... that the air is full of helpers ... that in every moment I may choose bliss. Her rivers penetrate all of life.

"I am the source of life," says Joy: "Each person's journey is a dance with me—losing, finding, sadness and elation—wandering the course of the intimate river. You who have encountered early abduction or abuse are on a journey of rediscovery: 'Where did they take your joy? Where have they hidden her?' This is no idle task for you must find me—I demand to be found! I am the river of life. Sap, juice, kundalini, chi ... you cannot live without me."

Authentic joy is the nemesis of domination—and so the empire crumbles as the river, laughing, erodes its foundation.... Do not be surprised at this.

Strange, that it is easier to trust pain than joy.

We are learning.

Tell me more about joy.

She is here now, in her aspect of sweetness, asking nothing but quietly radiating. Feel her warmth. She does not tire, as she is constantly self-renewing. Imagine a rushing mountain stream whose source is divine ecstasy. Imagine school-children bursting out of closed rooms into sunlight with wild shouts of life. Imagine a forest floor in springtime covered with more new shoots than the eye can see....

Is there a beginning and end to wind, or waves, or sunlight? A small bird angles and swoops with abandon, trusting the wind and its own perfect form, held within swiftly changing elements in blissful balance. This is Joy.

There is one joy, and it is the flower of the awakened heart.

On a Glad Spring Day

You feed me today with sweet breezes and the lilting songs of birds who've long awaited spring. We celebrate together, baked in sunlight, even though the air is still cool and snow patches linger in shady places. This is so good for my heart, Beloved. I long to do your work and live my days with you, but as you know I often become obsessed with little jobs, and computer-bound with a headache and my soul shut-down....

Now is the only moment, dear one. This joy wafting on the breezes, birthing in your sun-pressed heart.... This joy is all there is.

Is this what happens when the clouds have passed over the sun?

This is reality, Jane.

But the things that warm my heart right now are temporary: the land was covered with snow and ice not long ago, under a dark sky....

The seasons you experience throughout life offer an opportunity to penetrate the veil of the temporary show. Death also may appear to be a cold and dark place. But see how soon these illusions are replaced by birdsong and rejoicing? And so it is with the great cataclysms of this time, whether in Japan or Africa, the Middle East or here at home.

The Abiding Reality is this glorious transformation. And every year Nature repeats her show as if to say: "What do you think is really Real?" And remember as she lovingly repeats this grand performance, that you are the observer. You may also be the observer in your own life's cycles: "Ah—I am strong and happy now. Oh—today is a sad and tired day. Ah—the body is shedding itself now...." This observer-self is eternal. It is the materialism of this age which has taken away some of the breadth (we might say poetry) of this perspective. And we are here to offer joy in all the seasons. Because soon enough this body's life will pass. But we will always be here with you to celebrate this moment.

All that is Asked of You

The air outside is a warm bright blessing. The simplicity is gradually penetrating all parts of me and I begin to find my way within it, my regular work: this time with you, tending the household, maintenance of my other projects.... Do you have words for me today?

You are faithful. I would like you to absorb the importance of this, for this is all that is asked of you. It is your mind which heaps up other requirements and expectations. How confusing they are! How endless! They are mountains that cannot be climbed, that simply exhaust the pilgrim lost within them. Now you may leave such fruitless pursuits behind, "shake the dust from your feet" and take this simple journey with me.

Let us be like children, side by side, exploring the endless wealth of divine blessings. With the fool's voice we cry out: "There is always hope and light, healing and joy!" It is our secret, that this is true. There is no impediment to joy for those willing to pierce illusion with their simple attendance. Let them come to this class and they will see: the Teacher speaks everywhere, in every heart at every moment. "Simply listen. Now. Here. Be with me." This is all the Lover asks. Release your worries. Patience will reveal all mystery and undress all illusion. Open your heart and begin.

For the Reader:

Let joy have a word with you today and listen with your heart, knowing that she is already secretly singing inside of you. Offering yourself in silence, ask where joy is peeking out of the tired corners of your heart and of this world. Maybe she is waiting to be noticed and nurtured by you. If you encounter sadness or indifference, record your feelings and shower them with love.... Ask the Lover of your soul to help you. You are never alone.

... Offering yourself in silence, ask where joy is peeking out of the tired corners of your heart and of this world.

THE DIVINE PERSPECTIVE

"When tigers of worries, sickness and death are chasing you,
your only sanctuary is the inner temple of silence."
—Paramahansa Yogananda, *Where There is Light*

Comfort in Tragedy

It is one thing to find peace in relatively quiet times—the test comes when something tragic has happened to us or to someone we love. The following message came to me in meditation for a young friend who lay unconscious in the hospital after a terrible car accident:

You must believe the truth of this situation. We speak only truth. Would the Lover lie about life and death and what is real? You have inherited the mental ignorance of this material realm. But within you there is another, finer realm, where Truth is found. This is the realm of the Abiding Spirit, where a soul finds comfort even as the body appears in great distress. This boy is held within Abiding Consciousness. Here all is whole and all is well. The soul receives great attention from spiritual helpers and loved ones. He is never alone.

Here he is unaware of the wounds of his material body—they are not part of his consciousness (any more than we feel wet when the rain has passed, or cold when winter is gone.) He is within the eternal energy realm which is here now, but invisible to our material eyes. It is a realm more real in every way than human consciousness can grasp. This abiding domain encompasses the material world, and surpasses it.

Imagine that the five faculties of touch, taste, sight, smell and hearing are in every moment a confusing din, distracting from the abiding frequencies of the Real. Stillness and the inward consciousness open a portal to true perception. When the physical body experiences great distress or death, the inner self may feel confusion: "Why am I so calm and peaceful? Why do I feel light and free of pain? Where am I?" Helpers come. It is not a fairy tale that tender helpers soothe and minister to each new soul who sheds mortal body-consciousness.

And so this friend is held and shown a world in every way more wonderful than the one we perceive with mortal senses. It is here now, this world. We are here. We are always here.

This life is a learning ground, a school. Great advancement can come with consistent effort. But it can be a very tough school. That is why so many souls shed their mortal body with relief and joy: "Now I see true beauty; now I hear the song of everything; now I feel lightness and bliss!"

Light in Times of Darkness

Let us speak to you about Light. Everything, in every moment, is laced with Light. Do you know this? Every shadow is evidence of the sun. Light is the form of creation, the building block of all that is. Feelings of despair come because you now see in part, you see "through a glass darkly."

War and suffering come when human beings feel disconnected from one-another. The answer is the true perception that we are One.

Why must we go through such darkness to learn?

We have spoken about time's illusion—that truth resides within the limited perception of this moment. Actually, what is true is the eternal manifestation: Hiroshima City as a temple of peace, Auschwitz as an opportunity for mercy. The vessel must be hollowed out, or hallowed. Only the hallowed vessel may be filled with divinity. It is true that all is Light, only Light.

A momentary perception proclaims process as reality, as if you saw the waves recede and claimed: "It is always low tide, the shore littered with detritus." In one moment, this is true. But in another moment the same space is bubbling with fluid life. Sometimes a tree appears dead, its crumpled dressing strewn about its base. But soon enough abundant green adorns its branches.

We cannot cling to death as anything more than process. And similarly we cannot seize the temporary manifestation even of amazing suffering as more than a passing show. How do we hold this understanding? Only with the unshakeable conviction of light and more light, love and more love. Because that is the abiding reality: Love is all that IS.

Guidance for a Worried Parent

Spirit friends: please speak about a child who is a great concern to his parents.

We are here. What we know you cannot yet know. What we can say is that you are enough. Your parental love is enough for this incarnate soul. His journey is his own deep mystery. Do you know the voice of the sap in the pine trees or the maples? Do you understand the deepest journey of any other living being? Regard each life with reverence, however it may baffle or frustrate you.

What do I do with my fear and frustration?

Offer them to the altar of our union. Seek our union in the sunlight and in the shadows, trusting the mystery of this life. Teach your children (beginning with the ones inside of you) to trust this mystery. What else can you do?

This is the impulse that increases Love's breath within the universe. It begins with this willingness to offer love, regardless of all evidence to the contrary. Treat every human relationship as an opportunity to increase love and you will begin to enter the sacred circle where holiness is unbroken. It is possible. Indeed, it is the truth of what is: all is holy. Remove the veil. Believe it. The scales will fall from your sight more freely with your cooperation.

A Rare Confession

What comfort is there for one who is currently suffering?

What do we say when you are suffering? We are here. We accompany you in this earthly vibration, this world at war for lack of human tenderness and understanding, this place whose inhabitants do not yet perceive themselves one organism and therefore may obliterate another population ... or watch them starve on the evening news. We sit beside you in incomprehension of these phenomena. For now we know that all is one loving whole.

How painful it is to watch this show, this dreadful human drama. For us, sometimes there is weeping and there is discouragement. This is a rare confession. We too grow disheartened by the incomprehensible ignorance of life on earth. We do not say these words to comfort you. No. We sit beside you, our gaze downcast and our hearts heavy. For joy is so close at hand. We see you dear ones dying in a desert of your own creation when all around you are cisterns of living water. And sometimes we weep. Even though we know that all will be renewed in time and that this too will be redeemed, we weep. You are all so precious to us.

Those of us who speak to you are of an order or school that closely interacts with mortal life. We wish to be in this communication—to provide reminders of divine possibility, to offer direction, to comfort the grieving. We align our energies with the human vibration in order to communicate. In so doing—as if we were connecting electrical circuitry—we give as well as receive your pulse. We are attuned to your conditions. We accompany you like unseen friends, quiet companions.

It is a lovely work, and one which you may choose to do on leaving your body. But we cannot say that it is without pain. And perhaps in this moment that is what your soul is asking to know. Are we, as divine messengers, indifferent, because we know the outcome? And now you have your answer. We feel your heartache in our hearts. We weep with those who weep. We bewail with you the darkness, even though we know the dawn is here.

For the Reader:

What are the dark places in your life? On this piece of paper or in your journal, in the secret intimacy of your quiet time, ask the Beloved to speak with you about these painful places. Then empty your mind of answers and focus on breathing and waiting. When an image or a word comes, record it without judgment. Be open to what Love is trying to say. You may be surprised by the beauty that emerges from your listening heart....

*... Ask the Beloved to speak with you about these painful places. Then empty your mind
of answers and focus on breathing and waiting. When an image or a word comes,
record it without judgment.*

WAR: LOVE HAS MANY FACES

"Let each know that it is a harp upon which the breath of God would play. As seekers after divine guidance be uplifted; and thus may ye hasten the day when war will be no more."

—Edgar Cayce

"Your solitude will bear immense fruit in the souls of men and women you will never see on earth."

—Thomas Merton

What can I do?

For sensitive souls, the violence of this planet often feels unbearable. We ask ourselves: "What can I do with my own isolated efforts, my own small heart?"

I have been inspired to use creativity to help transform the human perception of an enemy or outsider. With the use of drama I entered the realm of Auschwitz to speak the loving vision of Etty Hillesum, who died there. Years later I visited Hiroshima to create an exhibit of collage portraits of atomic bomb survivors who offer their memories as a plea for nonviolence. But in my quiet conversations with spiritual companions a new way was opening.

Overwhelmed by violence in the Middle East, I began asking what help I might offer from the quiet of my room. For the next several days I was guided into four moving encounters that illustrate how a willing heart can accompany someone on the other side of the world as they experience terror and even transition out of the body. I now believe that if this experience can happen to me, it is available to anyone.

Holding in Compassion: the Middle East

There is tension in my chest for the anguish of a new war with fresh suffering and death. What legacies will such losses yield? How can I hold and even help such distant suffering?

Beloved: rest in me. We are together in the center of life. There is no distance. The Lebanese child who is extinguished is your child, as is the young Israeli soldier aiming the weapon your child.

I feel powerless to help.

Consider that. Consider that my power is all, and that you and I are one. The illusion of powerlessness is a great trick to obscure the unfathomable power which is your birthright in me. Your child who seems to perish in Lebanon is eternal. Even now you may comfort her to ease the passing, reminding her that there are beautiful angels to bathe her wounds.

The soldier-child needs more of your compassion. How complex the suffering here. Hold him as you bear together all the struggles of this life. Give him a safe, non-judgmental space.

If you are willing, I will bring them to you. This will be your service.

There is silence, then I begin to have a subtle perception—an inner sensation, as if someone is with me in great fear—an Israeli civilian?

Hold her.

As I wait, I sense terror—missiles, explosions ... everyone is so frightened. It is too much to bear.

Hold and feel with this woman. Grieve for the sorrow and the waste, even as you know that this is a temporary play upon the vast, eternal stage. Her destiny is not here ... her future will hold peace and joy and everlasting love.

Now it is inhumane, unbearable.

Yes. But you are sharing a moment of peace now, beyond all distances—a moment of deep communion in divine compassion. Something of eternal beauty exists here.

It doesn't seem like enough.

How do you know? The mysteries of the soul's journey are great. You are not in charge of knowing. But I am asking you to hold her. We are holding her together.

Remember only this: there is no time or distance. We are altogether now in perfect bliss for all eternity. Here there is no pain, no hunger, only the love each heart yearns for. To hold another in this place of bliss—even for a moment—is a perfect offering. Could there be any more beautiful activity than this? How sweet the fragrance of our love.

Thank-you.

A Second Day of Compassionate Holding

Shall I be with someone who is suffering now—will you bring them to me?

I will.

Soon I begin to feel the presence of a woman who is barely alive. It is not only her body which is mortally wounded, there is also anguish in her soul and heart. She seems to rest across my lap, as still as an altar, as if poised between death and life.

What I perceive is that she is being gently decorated with jewelry and fine cloth made by the loving hands of women who have combed the ashes for hope. They carefully paint the colors of worship between her brows and make soft music, retelling the story of her childhood, her young womanhood, her children ... honoring and adorning her for the triumphs of this life.

I am confused now. It seems that she is before me, seeing me and thanking me. And then I cannot perceive her at all. I perceive nothing.

(pause)

What do I need to understand today, in order to go out into the world?

Remember that it is a dance. A play. A story told and then forgotten. The existence with me is all. What does the story matter? The murderer who finds me is also my beloved. The cruelest heart can find her way to me. The story is a thin veil, useful in that it is a pathway to my door—the doorway of consciousness, past which no stories are needed.

You are telling me such wonderful things today! I am so grateful.

We are together. This increases the joy everywhere, even in this lovely Iraqi woman who has just passed.

A Third Encounter

I am asking to be given the grace to serve—perhaps again to hold someone from the Middle East.

After some stillness, this is what I begin to perceive: a scene of great anger and violence ... someone being beaten. I feel outside if it and totally powerless.

I am guided to insert myself—as divine energy—into the center of the violence, so that each assailant faces me. I sit down in their midst. They are frightened and do not know what to do. They seem to disperse.

A boy is left lying on the ground, face down. It feels desolate: the life is passing from him. I do not know what to do and so I wait with him, not disturbing his body in any way and yet protecting him. It feels important that nothing disturb this vigil.

He wakes up and feels great fear and confusion. It is his spirit which is waking, but he doesn't understand this—he feels frantic. I surround him with divine energy so that as he struggles he finds only the peace that I embody for him.

He is 10 or so, and has held raw emotion for much of his difficult life, perhaps in a Palestinian camp or settlement. Now there is no more hunger or anxiety. Together we hold the sorrow of his short life, giving it all the serious attention it deserves. They treated him like a boy and so he played the part, but his life held scarcely any ease or joy. Even as an infant, his great eyes were vigilant.

Time passes. I ask: "Is it safe for me to let him go?"

You cannot let him go, he is with you now. It will take some time for him to find his mission here. He will be well.

Thank-you.

The Fourth Day

I am wishing again to engage in this compassionate time with you today: will you bring me someone to me?

I will.

After a long wait I have what seem odd perceptions, as if I were speeding through the air ... riding in a tank ... walking through flat land. I hold these images and begin to grasp a sort of collective spirit of the American Military—mechanical, precise. There is comfort in this communal identity—a family whose father is a military commander and whose mother is America, whose siblings are the brothers and sisters in arms.

Shall I be with them?

Yes. Hold them, feel them ... offer yourself to them. Be still in their presence.

I feel myself beside a young officer making some sort of routine journey. Looking this way and that, his mind is focused on the usual business. I try offering him my energy, but there seems to be no connection. Then I experience crazy, uncomfortable feelings. Everywhere there is chaotic energy with no center. I think perhaps there has been an explosion.

I cannot connect with the soldier amid the violence. Then there is a sense of despair as he begins to discover he is no longer an entity: there is no localized body, only odd energetic tremors. Slowly I begin to perceive the shape of the man in a new form—carrying no material weight, but somehow recognizable as an entity.

An old man comes to him, perhaps his grandfather, who had loved him as a boy. He holds the man-child who is so frightened. "It's all right ... it's all right ... I will help you sort this out," he says. The young man is stunned. I have the sense of his soul needing so much work to be healed.

The Center of Each Heart

I wonder if today again there will be a distant encounter. After about a half hour of calming my mind and 'tuning in,' I sense a sort of luminosity behind my closed lids: spiritual presence has come to join me.

Are we ready to receive someone?

We are shifting and transforming energy even now—no specific work is necessary.

Speak to me, Lord.

We are together here. Be still. I have something to say.

The sky is listening, the trees are listening, the still fox in the woods is listening, even the insects are listening....

I am working everywhere in the world. In the center of each heart, each atom, every particle of everything, I exist. I Am. Here before you now, I Am. I Am the heart that seeks me and I Am the beloved who is sought. There is nothing which is apart from me.

But what about abuse, disease ... war?

What about them?

They are wrong and horrible. Am I to perceive them differently?

When you have experienced connection with the lives of these four people in these last days—people in the midst of war—what have you felt?

The first was terrified....

And?

And I held and quieted her—we both felt an exchange of the comfort of god-presence.

And?

It was beautiful.

And then?

The woman, grieving and dying....

What did you experience with her?

She was adorned and lovingly ministered to—it was beautiful. She seemed to thank me as she passed on.

Then?

The scuffle, and the little boy. The fight was full of anger, but as I stood there, in the center, it dissipated. The little boy needed to be held and protected as his energy assimilated and transferred itself.

And?

And then he was fine.

Then?

Yesterday, the soldier. I think he was blown up. We helped him make the transition. The old grandfather came to this young man when he had crossed over.

Yes.

I see that when we are there together there is no darkness or absence of love.

Yes.

I get that you are saying it is only perception which tells me there is a godless place or time. But at the same time I don't get it. What about Auschwitz, Hiroshima? Ask Elie Weisel: there was no God in his recollection. What about the hell of the A-bomb survivors?

What did you feel at Auschwitz?

That it was the saddest and holiest place on earth.

What did Etty Hillesum feel in the transport camp?

"God is in safe hands with us, despite everything."

Still I cannot believe this. I think of the mother in my exhibit of Hiroshima survivors, who found her son at last, his burns covered with maggots, dying a slow death because there was not enough medicine. He was 15.

I am glad that you want to understand: this is very precious to us.

Who are you?

We are love, light, pure being. We are outside of time and space and body, and also utterly within these forms. We are helpers.

What I'm getting is that while in this visible dimension suffering happens, there is also the reality of your complete healing infusion, at the same time. But the suffering still happens … no?

What is suffering?

Suffering is terror, pain, hunger, despair, hatred … not feeling you. Emptiness, loss, confusion…. It hurts me to hold all these definitions of suffering and wait for your words.

Why does it hurt?

Because I don't get it! I don't get what you are saying to me. It doesn't feel real enough to face down all this pain.

Are you willing to listen?

I am. *(long pause and struggle)*

You are trying too hard. I am right here, pouring the answer into your heart. Receive….

I am holding the starving Jews of Bergen Belsen, watching their loved ones go up in smoke. I can't trivialize suffering!

Do you think that I am trying to trivialize suffering?

I don't know.

The only dance is love, and it has many faces, offering itself everywhere. The deeper the wound the richer the infusion of sacred balm, as you have experienced over these past days. For every loss there is breath-taking mercy and restoration beyond imagining. There are realms of love only known to those in dire extremity. Love has many faces.

Are you saying Auschwitz is a face of love? Hiroshima? I don't understand!

Every point on the earth is divine emanation. Every atomic particle is the center of God. God loving, knowing and rejoicing in God-self is the pleasure song of the universe. The absence of God is like a dream—always, in awakening, there is relief: "Ah yes, this is what is true."

For a long time people or groups may seem to sleep, living their lives in ignorance and confusion. And that is also perfect, for in waking they are filled with fresh joy and bliss. The nature of truth and perfection does not change.

Everywhere Love will bloom. She is even now sowing seeds and putting forth tender shoots. She is fiercer and stronger and far more enduring than all the storms in her way.

What shall I do—how shall I help this earth "groaning in travail?"

Help by being who you are—by affirming your presence here, and breathing. Feeling and breathing. I will do the rest.

For the Reader:

It is easy to feel overwhelmed by the news we hear of the world, which is usually the bad news. (How we need to hear of all the miracles that are constantly taking place!) Just for a few moments, please take the time to focus on one issue that feels sad and discouraging to you. You may write it down, and write the feelings that you have.

Now ask for the divine perspective. You may write: "Please help me!" or "What can I do?" You may place your hands over your heart and feel the warmth. Offer time for the seed of Love to expand in your heart and ask: "What are your words for me today?" You may be moved and surprised by the beauty that comes.

You may also try asking if there is someone you can help today by holding them in your heart. It may be someone you know, or your heart may be drawn beyond your own experience. Be very tender with yourself as you attempt this, for it is holy work.

... Take the time to focus on one issue that feels sad and discouraging to you. You may write it down, and write the feelings that you have. Then Offer time for the seed of Love to expand in your heart and ask: "What are your words for me today?"

... Take the time to focus on one issue that feels sad and discouraging to you. You may write it down, and write the feelings that you have. Then Offer time for the seed of Love to expand in your heart and ask: "What are your words for me today?"

PRESENCE

"To drink at the Source of all that lives and breathes expands the heart and makes the blood sing, echoing the song of all the vital fluids in the world."
—Jean-Yves Leloup

All There Is

Do you have a message for me today?

Of course. I am with you. This conversation is our beautiful dance. I wish to free you from the many worries of your nature—money, worth, future, work.

You have my attention.

Listen: work is this place we inhabit and create together. There is nothing else but this.

The need for exercise, discipline … income, accomplishments?

I repeat: there is nothing apart from this conversation. Your mind alone creates the illusion of separate 'work.' All being is one being—our conversation is all there is. There is nothing apart from this.

What??

You will understand. Give it time. Now be still and listen....

(pause) **I have been turning the Atomic Bomb into beauty and closeness, and Auschwitz into hope and inspiration. I have been learning to hold pain and darkness until they yield a diamond and a pearl ... this out of my conversation with you.**

Yes. And so we are ... and so we inhabit all energy before, during and after such transformations. There never has been or will be anything that is apart from our dance, our conversation.

This comes in and out of focus for me.

Let go. Do not think.

Easy for you to say!

Hold me.

... I perceive you stretched across my lap, embodying all of the love and striving and pain and hope of the world.

Now let me hold you. Imagine me as a loving circle of women ministering to your needs—comforting your sorrow, sharing your joy, holding your struggling path. Imagine that this is all there is: me in your arms, and you encircled by my nurturing love.

What about all the rest? Iraq, Africa ... the broken dishwasher, the bills?

Begin to take the initiative, dear student, to choose what you perceive. Some of this will be your choice. You will see what you choose to see. Please cooperate with this process.

Thank you for being patient with me.

You Are the Door

Almost as soon as I sat down in my meditation room today, I began to feel ease and joy. This is my true life, my being. Oh, beloved: help me to shed the rest! Help me in directing my intention towards dwelling in this being-state. And when I feel the other selves—ego-selves—let me easily refocus, as if my vision were temporarily out of focus.

It brings us sweet joy to be together. And you see how little effort is involved: a slight shift of the inner eye, a relocation of focus. Now I have words for you. Listen.

I am listening.

Today we are one. The ascent and the descent are one. The door opens before you to true Presence. Do you wish to enter?

I see that I am a bit frightened, clinging to self-protection.

Yes. What you are asking of me can only be done by you.

Help me to understand. I feel foggy.

Be still for a moment.

... I see that I have the opportunity—now—to be in God's presence continually.

Yes, within yourself.

How do I find the door?

You are the door. This self, with all of its limitations and illusions, is the doorway to blissful consciousness.

How?

Ask yourself, each time you feel pain or frustration: "What is the truth of this moment?" Try it.

Now I feel a scattered, vague, doubtful, a bit off-base and guilty.

Ask yourself...

What is the truth of this moment?

... Fear.

Absorb this gift of revelation.

There is a vast amount of fear. Personal fear, self-doubt, global insecurity ... terror, frailty.

Can we name this feeling "Fear Identity?"

Yes.

Do not attempt to dispel Fear Identity. Hold it close to your heart, as if it were a small child or a tiny animal, disoriented by terror. Simply hold it close for a moment.

Who are you now?

I am the one who comforts the fearful one ... like a patient, loving mother.

Look around you now—who is with you?

The holy ones ... the eternal helpers…. **Oh, my!**

Yes.

Thank-you!

For the reader:

As a pleasant exercise, use the space provided here to try the simple exercise of sitting in a comfortable position, taking a few relaxed, deep breaths, and asking yourself: "What is the truth of this moment?" Taking all the time you need and holding yourself tenderly, record the thoughts that come, and then reflect on them with love and acceptance....

... Use the space provided here to try the simple exercise of sitting in a comfortable position, taking a few relaxed, deep breaths, and asking yourself: "What is the truth of this moment?"

THE ETERNAL MOMENT

"There was a young lady named Bright
whose speed was much faster than light.
She went out one day
in a relative way
and returned on the previous night."

—Anonymous

Who in this culture is not affected by the endemic nature of stress? This societal addiction can rob us of peace, hope and joy. But if we can allow ourselves to be still and let the waves of anxiety wash over us, we may find ourselves at the gates of divine peace.

Divine Perspective

Dear friends: please help me with the stress that seems to wait for me as I awaken in the morning, feeling right away that there is not enough time to relax in stillness. Please give me your perspective.

Let us address this issue of time. Anxiety and perfectionism stem from perceiving time within a container, bounded on either side by illusions of Now and Then, Yesterday and Tomorrow. The "unforgiving moment" can become an oppressive tyrant to the soul trapped within this pattern of perception. Imagine for a moment that there is no boundary—no today or tomorrow, no now and then—only one eternal moment where all time is present. See how this relaxes anxiety about performance and accomplishment? In this way you may take up the threads of last year or next month, for the perception that they are discrete and separate from this moment is erroneous. Smooth the edges of an old encounter, rehearse the joy of a future reunion. Hold these within this present experience.

How foolish, for example, to map the waters of the ocean—to chart the waves, which are here one moment and there the next. The ocean is one continuous inter-relational body. Time is similarly organically united. Can you map and measure wind? No: because its subtlest origins are indistinguishable from its mightiest manifestations. It is without beginning or end. This comprehensive understanding sheds a gentler light on each changing circumstance, for what seems a tragedy today may bear blessings for tomorrow. Hiroshima City exists now as a beautiful living monument to world peace. Auschwitz holds the healing prayers of countless visitors and symbolizes a powerful lesson in the abiding human spirit. Time viewed in its segregated increments is illusory. Perceive the possibility of blessing now: embrace misfortune as a pregnant seed.

As you release your grasp on momentary perfection, you allow eternity to fertilize each circumstance. Practice this, for it will relax and open your soul to divine blessing in every 'now.'

The Greater Reality

I'd love to hear from you, my companions. We haven't spoken for a while.

We are here, dear one. And we appreciate your noticing the need to be present in this moment. Life is so much simpler and more joyful in this way. Here, together, just as we are and will be for all time. Because all time is now. When we shift our focus to the bliss and radiant joy that's eternally present, then we can gently observe the passing phenomena of physical bodies and all of the events that befall them.

What we also wish to stress is that it is entirely all right to distance yourself, as needed, from the emotional and material vicissitudes of this life. This is not laziness or denial. It is in fact tuning into the Greater Reality—that all will be well. The trials are part of the passing show, forms of 'work' taking place all around you that may serve the karma of evolution. For you to over involve yourself with all of this may actually be detrimental.

Let us give you an analogy: in the world of sustainable farming, the steward of the land notices season after season that what appears as blight to one crop benefits another, or that what appears as a pest one year fertilizes a new crop-strain in the next. Within the perspective of time, the farmer begins to understand that the self-correction of natural cycles possesses a higher wisdom than his own temporal awareness can perceive. By respectfully observing the behavior of organic life over time, the farmer learns to support its cycles. The land teaches its steward.

Often personal crises are part of a self-correction process that ought not to be disturbed. But with our limited vision we may fail to grasp this. A humble approach tells us that we are not possessed of the eternal view: we do not know the plan of God, of Love, the Big Picture. So to observe with patient assurance is often the best approach.

Offering Time

Today again we are speaking about time. We are experiencing the delicious expansive vista that can emerge as you offer your time unconditionally. What a simple offering! Sitting comfortably, you can say within your thoughts: "I am releasing possession of my time. Here it is…." You give time. It is a beautiful doorway to ecstatic union which begins also with a gentle release of fear.

We can see how Fear and Time are kindred concepts—kindred illusions, it might be said. Fear presupposes a lack of purpose and love in creation. And Time, although in itself a benign measuring tool, often evokes feelings of scarcity. Examine the statement: "I don't have enough time." There is no limit to the Now. Moments are immeasurable within eternity. Only in possessiveness do we feel the need to measure time. What I do not have enough of is not mine to begin with! Since when did I possess this moment? And so is it not the loving gesture to return time—to say, "Here I am … here is my being within this eternal Now"?

Notice the deepening of breath as you release possession of time. It is akin to releasing fear … akin to sleeping peacefully within the arms of an all-caring parent who is vigilant in love and provision. This is the condition of grace which we messengers offer in every moment to you who seek spiritual union and freedom from the cares of this world. So offer time, and offer fear … and rest in the arms of the Beloved whose greatest desire is to hold you safely forever.

For the reader:

Try this gentle practice of offering Time:

As if a good wind were blowing, clean the storerooms of the mind: release all tension about this moment, the one before it, or the next. Maybe as you experience this cleansing wind a lot of other cares that crease your brow will fly right out the window and find themselves perched on a nearby tree, or floating with the breeze.

Our unseen friends are asking us to lighten the load. If worries come to you as you meditate, you might give them little balloons to hold as they fly above the clouds.

What do we really own here and what do we really know? Why not try lightening the load? It may be that the baggage we carry keeps us from rushing into the arms of the living God.

In the space provided, record the feelings that come as you release fear and the concept of linear time.

... In the space provided, record the feelings that come as you release fear and the concept of linear time.

In the space provided, record the feelings that come as you release fear and the concept of linear time.

HUMOR FOR THE JOURNEY

"Angels can fly because they take themselves lightly."
—Anonymous

Sometimes when we feel weighted down by the intensity of the human journey, the mysteries of the natural world consort to show us the humor in our situation, and this can be a great gift.

The Messenger

That red-winged blackbird seems to smash himself against the glass until I awaken. When I'm watching—no smash. But when I lie back down and drift off to sleep … crash, bang, smush. I sit up and look, and there he is, filling up his wide chest, pulling back his wings and crying out. Is he some cosmic messenger?

It works, in any case. He crashes till my tired, grumpy self can't stand it anymore and I at last sit up for good. And then perhaps the cardinal comes (the lesser birds respectfully back away). His plume aloft, he surveys the handsome landscape and I think: "So—life is still worth living."

If this whole performance is meant to prop me up it's working. Now I have my tea. I've hobbled downstairs (listing from side to side and inwardly counting up the aches in hip, foot, back and head). I've cleaned the kitchen, fed the cat and given him his antibiotic, made my precious tea and returned to bed. But I am sitting up.

Are you calling me inward, Beloved? Are you, in the voice of the blackbird and the splendor of the cardinal, saying: "Wake up, sit up, be here now?" I am here now, my love. And I declare that in all this world nothing is more important than this conversation—this silence—with you.

On Taking Yourself So Seriously

Today I am feeling mired in self-doubt and asking for words of guidance on my path.

We thank you who work in the name of Love for your tenacity and your faithfulness. We thank you for your offerings. Now—in the name of God— receive our grateful love and resist the habit of self-doubt. Allow gratitude and rest and remember to smile often: this is your plenty!

Laugh at yourself also. Laugh at what a silly mess a human can make of any situation, just as you would laughingly enjoy the confusion of a kitten wound up in a ball of yarn, or a child shrieking at a game of hide-and-seek.

From our vantage point, this is a level of reality we wish to impart. You all take your lives awfully seriously for beings whose brain has no idea where they have come from or where they are going and who live so rigidly by the mythology of each passing era. We uphold your earnest efforts, and we also offer humor as a tonic for many ills brought on by fear and misconception. It is not as serious as you think!

Now you may consider with a smile the humor of your situation: you ardently wish to serve, but when you push too hard you stumble over your own feet! You wish to honor heaven, and the earth slaps you in the face! What is useful to notice in this situation? We cannot escape the form of our lives. The mass of matter cannot be denied, however temporary. For every rabbit a magician pulls out of a hat, there is a hut full of dung. Do you see? We must deal with ordinary reality—it is our milieu. It is our temporal home. Welcome to Earth!

The mystery has a sense of humor. It is a comic tragedy performed on a temporary stage within a glorious eternal cosmos. But if the actors do not focus on their part, they forget their lines and blocking and stumble over their own feet. To attempt to escape to eternal realities in a sense undermines the purpose of the show. What is the purpose of the show? Ah, that is the mystery. Perhaps each player discovers the purpose in their dedication to their own part.

Ask yourself: What is my part? How might I enjoy it, taste and appreciate it? This is self-love. You forget the importance of self-love. It is a doorway to so much joy. Out of joy flows sweet service which will not strain the servant.

You will see that the dance is one of mutual enjoyment. Please take time to absorb this. Now we suggest that it would be useful to take a walk. There will be time to worry later in the day!

A Cosmic Joke

I guess where I keep getting derailed is with a sense of ambition about this writing: it should feel important, significant.

This amuses us, because it is a sort of cosmic joke.

Do tell.

…that every effort at success and glory fails in the end. It's the effort at no effort, or the abandonment of effort, that is fruitful. But how does one try not to try? It's the cosmic maze: because in a sense the only predictable outcome is failure. And the only cure for failure is forgiveness. But you cannot try too hard at forgiveness or it becomes an effort, which will fail. So it's just being here now, whiling away the time in conversation with invisible energy. And, of course, meeting the human animal's physical needs.

We laugh with delight, not derision, because we have come here in love and humility to accompany you on this baffling and wonderful journey. And we are well acquainted with its illusions.

What you are doing is enough. This is why we often suggest resting. This is how the pace works. Within the prevailing culture one feels a need to make excuses for resting and taking quiet time apart. To be busy seems the imperative, in spite of the uselessness of the pursuit. This pattern is often unhealthy, and it may require some souls to lean in the direction of exaggerated stillness to begin to restore balance. Many are now called to such periods of contemplation, and to them we send strong encouragement: this is an important contribution.

I want to remember to be grateful for all that I have, all the blessings.

Yes.

My family, friends, food, shelter, health … this conversation: I am so grateful for this!

And you will see how great it is in time. When you come to the end of this life the accomplishments will seem less important than who you are as you stand naked before the Source: All-that-is. Then it is only this bare soul, and here our conversation will have been a great gift and jewel. We will be beside you, and you will know us. You will have helped others also, mostly by being true to your path and your divine heart.

It seems strange to contemplate the end of my life.

It won't be so very long before that time is here. To hold that knowledge close to your heart now will help to clarify your path each day. The term of this life is short in the perspective of eternity. But each moment you may dwell in eternal bliss as you shift your gaze to the divine conversation. It is so simple and so close at hand. We are here.

For the Reader:

Humor is a fine tonic for the ills of this Earth school. Perhaps the Beloved will have a gentle laugh with you this morning. Are you taking it all too seriously? Sometimes, in order to gain peace and perspective amid the pressures of this life, we might need to visit the end of it. There, as the soul frees itself from the mortal garment, what will be truly important? What wounds will not be soothed by the gentle hands of eternal helpers?

Ask the Lover to give you a giggle or a good laugh today, and write about it. Let this be the beginning of a collection you can return to when you have forgotten how to laugh.

... Ask the Lover to give you a giggle or a good laugh today, and write about it.

INTERNAL ECOLOGY

*"Gratitude for the gift of life is the primary wellspring of all religions.
… It is a privilege to be alive in this time when we can choose to take part in the self-healing of our world."*

—Joanna Macy

Directions for these times

At a time when there is so much concern for the fate of the earth and its resources, I ask my guides for discernment. What is the role of each individual pilgrim?

Please speak to me about the changes that are occurring now.

What is true of the macrocosm is true of the microcosm. As the world seeks new forms of energy to power modern civilization, the individual looks internally for new energy sources. Both are entwined in the transformation of this era. What we wish to express now is perhaps a more subtle shift within each individual psyche:

Listen. *Listen to the silence. First hear the ambient sounds: airplanes, cars, wind, birds…. Then listen to the pulse of emptiness between these sounds.*

Breathe. *Breathe consciously. Let your mind join in the soft fluidity of environmental noises. Let the thoughts that occur join the pulsing sound of trains and birds and traffic….*

Release. *Release the tyranny of mental agenda. Let your inner eye—the doorway to your soul—grow softer. Let beauty be the gate-keeper. For too long a strict hand has ruled the mind, as if it were industrial chief to all internal operations. This Teutonic landlord is outdated now. Allow him a peaceful retirement. Now the vision softens, and the senses expand. The inner* *world is pregnant with a loving seed of transformation. What will grow from this seed? Who is this transformed human being? With patient awe let us await the birth.*

Miracles of life can only be held by the sweet hands of children and the very wise. Adopt child-mind. Transformation is at hand. It is safe to retire the strident inner voices that have cried out for productivity, achievement, success. We see the outer fruits of over-emphasis upon material consumption, competition, productivity ... but what are the inner fruits? Perpetual stress, dissatisfaction, self-criticism, depression, confusion. And might we agree that these are not the desired fruits of human life? Begin to practice the techniques of inner ecology. Like open-minded children, be willing to play with new toys. And soon enough you will discover familiarity with these toys and delight in the endless pleasure they bring.

Remember: shift is a sensitive, subtle process. Allow, receive, be still. You are doing just fine.

Do Not Doubt Yourself

Spirit friends: I am seeking words from you today about my life and my direction, feeling a bit lost.

We are here. We are always with you, till the end of time. Know that we surround you in love and attempt to open yourself to that love as often as you can. It is a faithful source of vital energy to the soul who is often a stranger in a strange land.

It's difficult to relax into stillness—I feel a bit antsy and peculiar.

We surround you with love and compassion, reminding you that this earth school is not an easy one. Who can find their bearings in such a place? One must drop the plumb-line deep and wait in stillness often. And it is important not to measure success or failure according to your passing moods, as if changing cloud forms could alter the sky.

Remember: we wait with you as you wait, and we serve you in the waiting. We have come for this service, so you may detect our pleasure as you allow yourself to surrender to stillness. For this we have assembled. This is our work.

You may regard your quiet time as a service to us, for that is also true. You give us pleasure as you allow this.

I feel dislodged within myself, a bit off-center.

There are many factors involved in the dynamics of this moment. We would say that you are indeed more porous now and that you pick up frequencies from myriad sources. That is why our time together is so important and beneficial. You are learning to hold a state of greater receptivity. This condition may itself require discernment as you ask yourself: "What is my obligation now? What is my work and my direction?" Many people all over the world find themselves at such cross-roads. You are 'bridge people' who offer your vessels for communication of significant changes in this moment.

We wish to say to you: do not doubt yourself. Do not doubt your guides and helpers, your path and your own voice. Do not doubt your intuition, even as you learn to refine it. This time together is safe time. Here we reassemble to hold up to the light each facet of the journey that is painful or challenging. Attunement and joy are one stroke of the same brush.

The human journey is a fierce trial of discernment. Here on earth, spirit-souls enter ungainly bodies with limited mental abilities and urgent physical needs. There is a great cacophony of agendas as human desires jockey for power. As you receive us—your spiritual messengers—you also attune in new ways to other energies. So it is required at this time to consult often with Source. That is, <u>your</u> Source.

Now you need to trust a journey that is clouded in unknowing. Your mind will catch up and assimilate, but it is best to allow some cognitive uncertainty even as your plumb-line rests at its own true depth. You will understand better soon enough.

Trust that as you seek Spirit first the rest will follow. Now you are asked to offer yourself to this classroom. This time that we share is the primary work. This is home base. Here—in the frequency of Love—the soul finds rest and succor: here the soul lays down its burdens and soaks in precious sustenance. Rest now in the tender care that surrounds you.

Practice Gratitude

The calling now is to soften internal judgment and open channels of receptivity. Often this begins with perception of what is close at hand but unobserved. Receive with gratitude your surroundings. In this grateful observation you may begin to detect the graces that surround you in daily life. What is good? What is a gentle, subtle blessing? Where is life going effortlessly and well?

So much attention is diverted to the 'squeaky wheel' that all the daily graces go unobserved. But here is the home of divine magic, in all the subtle details that cooperate within the tapestry of physical life. Here is the dance of creation, involving no effort on your part.

And as you open to the ever-presence of simple grace, you also soften your own availability to the flow of abundance that is at the heart of life. And, yes, this often requires spaciousness and time where you allow thoughts and agenda to clear a place for receptivity.

Please begin with a simple practice of gratitude. You will be surprised at how effective this practice will be. Begin to notice all that is bountiful and good in your world—kind friends, simple pleasures, clear sky ... abundant positive influences.

These practices will even deepen your breath, because you will be noticing it is not all up to you. You are not making this life happen. In fact, you are more like a leaf on a river that flows with myriad currents. You may subtly incline yourself in one direction or another, but other elements affect the conditions of the journey. Do you see? You are trying much too hard!

So relax and notice. That is all. Breathe, relax, and observe with gratitude the dance of life. This is the only way to travel.

For the Reader:

In the space below, begin to list the blessings of your life. Are you able to walk, or sing, or talk with a friend? What can you appreciate in your home and in the world outside your door? As you list each blessing that you notice, take a moment to thank the creative powers of the universe for each small or great gift. You may return to this list and add to it, and as you reread it let your heart be filled with abundance: there is so much blessing.

... In the space below, begin to list the blessings of your life. Are you able to walk, or sing, or talk with a friend? You may return to this list and add to it, and as you reread it let your heart be filled with abundance: there is so much blessing.

WHO AM I?

"Now is the time to know that everything you do is sacred"
—Hafiz

Identity

I begin the day asking a question that has been suggested as a rich source for meditation: "Who am I?" First on my list are the complaints and short-comings, but then I begin to notice more possibilities. I ask my unseen friends: "Who am I?"

It might be well to say, "Who are we?"

I'm listening.

We have come into this incarnation together. You were never alone. Now is the time to comport ourselves as one—that is, a collective whose boundaries the individual mind is unable to comprehend.

The mind is the tired old machine; Ego is now an outdated term. There is one being, one life. Who is the one who sees out through this body's eyes?

I don't know.

Could we say that one is Life?

What about the individual me, the one I think of as myself?

The skin is shedding. The caterpillar is sacrificing itself within the chrysalis.

So it is only Life that I am?

Only Life?

I will try to imagine that Life is looking out through these eyes.

Whose eyes are these?

Life's eyes, I guess.

Understand that this shift is impossible for the mortal mind to grasp.

Yes: I see that. Life sees that.

So this is the very threshold of awakening to collective consciousness.

There is perhaps a fear of losing myself.

... the dried snakeskin ... the bloated caterpillar?

Maybe I'm ready for it.

It is flight, freedom, ease. The butterfly is free to show us how.

I can only take sips of this new beverage.

Glimpses. You cannot stare wide-eyed at the sun.

Help me, beloved, to grasp that we—and all of life—are one. And that in this greater identity we do not lose our precious self, the story that is this mortal life.

It is never meant to be lost. It is the precious vehicle. Love and care for the body continue. Moods and various challenges continue. Perception gradually shifts from 'I' to a pronoun that does not exist in your vocabulary. Even 'we' is insufficient.

As often as possible, let the mind rest. Collective pain is gathered there. What you think of as your own pain is often old, societal. Without over-analysis, think of it as broken, just as external global systems may be viewed as outdated and dysfunctional. So when you identify with the mind it is as if you are looking out through broken glass. The ego mistakenly takes on this fractured identity.

Without trying too hard, allow your soul and heart to drift into the meditative question, "Who am I?" You may be surprised at what reveals itself as the momentary trappings are unwrapped.

A Blossom of God's Creation

On the porch ... Summer breezes and high tide. What is this restless spirit? Do I need to receive more love? Show me, dear spiritual companions. Show me how.

Perhaps, dear one, these restless spirits are not your own. Perhaps they come to you for love ... the way the way a butterfly attaches to a flower, sensing its sweet nectar from afar. Do you think that everything that comes to you or passes through you is yourself? Many visitors come in the course of a day, just as you are hostess to many guests in this appealing home.

How do you greet these restless spirits?

Indeed.

Tell them there is nothing to fear. There is enough love for all. God is big enough to house every ill and transform it. And you—servant of Love—are not responsible for providing healing. This is important for your strength and sanity, because the hungry spirits will come. How do you make yourself ready and hold your inner spaces open to the loving transformation of all that is unfinished? By recognizing that you are a sweet blossom provided by God.

I sense a problem here. There is only so much nectar at any time. I become depleted when I offer too much.

So here is a distinction: you are not the provider of anything. This is an important shift of perception.

I guess if I am a blossom of God's creation my role—on conscious level—is pretty much nothing. My role is to keep in touch with God.

Precisely. Like the flower, open yourself to sunlight and rain. Allow soft breezes to move you ... welcome this brief experience of being a flower blossoming now.

Pretty simple.

Indeed.

I sense contentment exists somewhere down this path. Even for my jumpy mind.

You will die, dear one. This one who is now a blossom will fade and fall. It is good to recall this, holding it to your heart as a talisman. The Lover is with you in this sojourn where individual perception tells you that you are not God.

But am I God?

Of course. The flower is God ... as is the butterfly seeking its sweetness. You mind cannot grasp these things, remember, because it is of mortal substance. Allow your heart to receive love. This is really the answer to everything.

For the Reader:

It is a rich exercise to ask the question, "Who am I?" In your quiet place today, you have space and freedom to explore any answer that comes to you and try on each one as it appears. Ask yourself: "Does this feel true?" Allow plenty of time to explore this rich inquiry. You may be surprised to find where the journey of exploration takes you.

In the space provided, simply write the question, "Who am I?" then give it time and see what comes....

... In the space provided, simply write the question, "Who am I?" then give it time and see what comes.

THE VOICE OF LOVE

"Do you wish to know your Lord's meaning in this thing? Know it well, love was his meaning. Who reveals it to you? Love. What did he reveal to you? Love. Why does he reveal it to you? For love."

—Julian of Norwich

Take Comfort

Spiritual friends: please speak to me! As usual, I am feeling inadequate, and somewhat unworthy of love.

Do you suppose we are keeping score? Life is not easy, and we are well aware of this. The first thing that should be ejected from the kingdom of the Self is perfectionism. There is no place for self-judgment, which is often fiercely at odds with the gentle direction of Love, the Self's true Keeper.

So when you feel these judging voices, offer the immediate reflex of tenderness. Say to them: "We are waiting for another voice." And then do listen, until Love's gentle song bubbles up from the streams of busy thought. The voice of Love is your truest guide.

I would like to hear the voice of Love now.

Love says:

Take comfort, mortal traveler: when you do not hear me, it is not your fault. My voice does not cry out in the busy marketplace. I do not wish to compete for your attention. But you must know that I am here. Everything you see, taste and touch has been born of my creative impulse. All of this world is part of my song. The key is to seek the singer of the song … then you will enter into the chamber of the Beloved.

And when you cannot seem to hear the voice of the Singer, do not try too hard. For it is Love's job to find you. Perhaps a space will come, a pause in your day, and someone will touch your shoulder kindly, speaking with my voice … or perhaps sorrow will come, and in your wounded heart you will feel unexpected comfort, and that will be the comfort of my love. Perhaps you will be tired from all of your efforts and you will sleep and sleep so deeply that in the morning you will awaken refreshed. And the one who is refreshing your heart is Love.

I am not trying to hide from you, my dear one. In this game of hide and seek, it is I who am the seeker, and it is the confusion of this world which lets you think that you are hidden. So when you long for the comfort and the joy of Love's presence, simply say: "Here I am, my love! Here I am and I am wanting you to find me now. I am longing for you above all."

Before very long you will feel me—with you, beside you, within you … for I am always here.

You Are Never Alone

As usual, I am coming to you with inner pain this morning.

We are grateful for this time with you. How sweet it feels to join in conversation. Nothing is more precious than this. Please remember that this is the Abiding Reality—this conversation. Nothing else remains at the end of the day. Bodies will grow fat or thin, finance will be easy or difficult, children will have good times and bad. Only this loving union is constant in its fruitfulness.

Great tragedies occur through history, and it is appropriate to grieve them. But even as we grieve let us remember that for every cavity of dense suffering there is a great infusion of Light whose beauty dazzles beyond all imagining. Such is the dance of life.

But what do we do with the temporal discomfort of suffering?

We are here with deepest understanding of human suffering. That is why you are never alone. Human beings are not capable of this existence in a solitary fashion. It is when we stand in companionship to hold life's tender mysteries that we feel the joyful presence of Divine Love. In this way the human family begins to know itself in its true beauty and expand the Light in the universe.

For the Reader:

We are used to listening to so many voices in our lives: the inner critic, the outer critics, the radio, television, computer.... For just a few moments, please listen to the voice of Love.

Imagine as you breathe and listen that there is one creative impulse, one vast organism. Imagine, in the words of Hildegard von Bingen, that you are *"a feather on the breath of god."* Can it be otherwise, if all is Love?

Record your feelings in this space, as you continue on this path of exploration. Here you are learning to trust the sweet conversation with the lover of your soul—a discourse that will never end. Take a few moments to ask: "What is Love saying to me today?"

... Record your feelings in this space, as you continue on this path of exploration.
Take a few moments to ask: "What is Love saying to me today?"

WORDS FOR THE PILGRIM

"Just sit there right now—don't do a thing, just rest.
For your separation from God, from love,
Is the hardest work in this world.
Let me bring you trays of food and something that you like to drink.
You can use my soft words as a cushion for your head."
—Hafiz

Direction

Dear Friends: please give me direction for this scattered mind today.

Please know that we are here with you in this room. You are not alone. It is good to seek guidance and comfort. You may look at this time as if you were traversing a high mountain pass in a sacred range. Your own vision is obscured by wind and weather, and you do not know the way to your destination. This moment on the path is the way. This is what we are trying to convey. You are right to wait and seek as you do. It does no good for the pilgrim to flail about and set out in every direction when the path is unclear. In spite of all the material comforts of your world, you are a pilgrim. And this is one of the things we love best about this journey.

In this society so many circumstances reinforce the demands of the material establishment, and this creates a painful tension. See this as your training ground. How can you represent the pilgrim's path within this consuming material establishment? The pilgrim's path, that is, of seeking in stillness. A calling that involves waiting on the unseen can seem insignificant within the dense din of planetary travail.

What we wish to underline is that this represents an extraordinary opportunity for spiritual growth on your appointed path. Contrary to what your mind may repeat to you about slothfulness, worthlessness or inactivity, you are preparing in every way for a holy work. This time of waiting and purification aligns you with your mission.

Are We All Here?

In my morning quiet, I am asking my unseen companions: please speak.

Let it come to you: this is the new lesson. Receive. Trust it will come. What is it that you are needing?

… a reassurance of my own goodness. Reassurance that all is well, in spite of my passing moods. Sometimes I wake up in the morning feeling so dark.

You are checking in with us, and we are never dark. If you listen to us all the time there will be less density and discouragement.

I feel as if I am learning to do this. It's getting easier. Can you give me more tips?

Imagine we're walking this path together. When you feel alone, stop for a moment and ask, "Are we all here?" And wait until you feel us. Just as if we were hiking a mountain trail together: you'd sit on a rock to rest and wait for your companions to catch up from time to time. The journey becomes a lighter one when we are sensing each other's presence. We take pleasure in each other's company and together we can appreciate every aspect of the climb, even the parts that seem arduous.

I understand.

Check in with us. Say: "How are you?" or "Is it OK with you?" The simplest acknowledgement of our presence alters your awareness from a singular to a collective one. We are here. We are always here. This journey can be a happier and more comfortable one. This is what we're offering you now.

Thank you. Are we all here?

We are.

Do you have more guidance for me today?

Gratitude is the magic element, the hidden treasure. This is the key to a rich life, and to all God's good gifts. Delight in this life as much as you possibly can. Enjoy good things. Love, and receive love. Offer your gifts to the world fully and freely. When you taste fear, hug it quickly and replace it with love and gratitude. Poor fear hasn't got a chance in such company!

Offer, offer, offer … this is what brings joy. When you cease to give, the waters become stagnant and run in upon themselves. Be a river moving forward. Practice gratitude, which embraces the unknown and welcomes what is beyond your scope. Leave off self-scrutiny once and for all. It inhibits delight and blocks the flow of Love's blessings … and why waste time with that?

Shepherd of My Life

The thought comes to me that I must learn to be a shepherd of my life and my resources. Perhaps as I doubt myself or go off in search of new projects, I leave my sheep to scatter. The tending is so simple a task that it escapes my notice, and I suffer the consequences.

This is good direction, dear one. Early on you were trained in self-criticism, and this is the part to modify. Now become aware of your goodness and sufficiency. Can this feel like enough … like abundance?

Sometimes the shepherd's days are uneventful. Perhaps it feels dull. But if she/he runs away in search of adventure or becomes consumed in worry or self-criticism, all may be lost. Some days are days of resting, maintaining, taking stock. In fact, most days are like that! Do you need to do more with your life, or is it simply a habit to keep pushing on for more?

Now the call is to marshal your forces. A new stage of life is at hand. Now more will come to you, right to your doorstep. You do not need to feel that you are lacking in any way. Notice the resources that are already here. How can you know them if you do not spend time noticing them in love and gratitude? Every morning you may survey and identify the flock: this is the work of a seasoned shepherd. This practice of shepherding will also align you with Divine Source, and power will come in gracious and surprising ways. You have not been the producer of this herd: it is God's. You have been set in its midst, to appreciate and to do your part. Here is also daily peace and joy. Here is abundance, right here in the midst of your flock.

Encountering Difficulties

Do you have guidance for me in these mornings when I wake up feeling dark and confused?

This 'pre-set' mode of self-punishment is not entirely bad: it can act as a spur to deeper questing, which in turn will bring greater clarity and peace. Find your center and try to be in communion there with Light, Love and Truth … this is all you can do. When thoughts come that this is not enough, remember where you are—at the center of the greatest military super-power the world has ever known, a place riddled with materialism and blinded by its own excess. A place where addictions abound: to pleasure, productivity, power, consumption. There are so many reasons why this is difficult and confusing. The things you consume may come from countries where there is great poverty, but those places have things this culture often lacks—community, humility, simplicity.

So please recall all that is being transmuted in your quiet self-offering. Love is what you offer. What more is there to do? What is more precious on this earth? The shepherd offers love, patience, space and time. Thank you. We know how difficult this can be.

What do I do with all these challenging internal voices?

Still them. Imagine that the flock has been spooked in the night, and the shepherd needs to reassure them with simple signals that all is well, there is nothing to fear.

Why do the sheep get spooked in the night?

Perhaps there is fear in the air, and they smell it on the wind. Perhaps they had a fearful dream, or thought a predator was near. The point is that the shepherd knows his job: to quiet and reassure the sheep, keeping them contented and at peace. In this state they can serve their own life's purpose. So it is with these human fears, dear one.

We know that the entry and exit of this mortal life are framed in glory. The newborn child arrives with special magic, delighting us with her excitement. And the weary traveler often meets his final release with gratitude and awe, beholding Love's greeting at the door. Who is to say what levels of light are revealed along the way, or at what moment in the path a pilgrim might round a corner to stand face to face with unmasked glory? Like a labyrinth, the human journey seldom takes a straight path, its twists and turns too confusing for the linear mind. The journey is the thing: the willingness to humbly walk a confusing path with gratitude and joy—this is heroism.

Trust the shepherd. And find the shepherd in you, because you do not know the way. And the way is not of such great importance in the end. Dwelling in relationship requires abandonment of agenda. It requires trust, patience and great hope. Discernment is crucial within this commitment to relationship: is this path loving and good? Is the shepherd good? Where is my North Star?

My North Star is here, in conversation with you, beloved friends.

So you may think of us as God's shepherds … and in turn you may be conscious of shepherding your own internal flock—those feelings, thoughts, and fears—in love and contentment. All is well. Take time for peace and stillness, for simplicity and emptiness. Your mission will always find you if you are available in this way. The shepherd gathers the day's "Manna," then—stilling and comforting the flock—offers them daily sustenance, as from the hand of God.

For the Reader:

Look at your life and the bounty of it. Take a few moments to notice and record the resources that have been placed in your care. Who depends upon you for encouragement, friendship or leadership? What is your daily responsibility? This is your flock.

Notice all that is going well: the family members and friends who are healthy and progressing in their lives, the work you do that is beneficial ... whether it involves cooking a meal, cleaning a room, or organizing a business convention. There is always something to be grateful for.

Allow yourself the space for contentment, breathing in the abundance of your life. Surely God's love is blessing you, and you are allowing fruit to blossom on this earth. The time you take in grateful observation nourishes your flock and all that your life touches.

... Look at your life and the bounty of it. Take a few moments to notice and record the resources that have been placed in your care.

... Look at your life and the bounty of it. Take a few moments to notice and record the resources that have been placed in your care.

THE NEW INDUSTRY OF THE TWENTY-FIRST CENTURY

*"May the Holy One preserve in me
a burning love for the world
and a great gentleness."*

—Teilhard de Chardin

The Alchemy of the Heart

Beloved: how blessed I feel this morning to sit in stillness and feel that we are together. Feeling you is everything, but so often I do not. Please speak to me about how to have the sure knowledge of your company, here and now.

It is a subtle awareness in your heart. Release any mental analysis: that is the place of doubt and separation. Let it go, as if you were watching clouds pass before the sun. Let it go and breathe. You may place your hands over your heart and allow sensations to come, sweetly welcoming them all. Imagine that we love you. Call us friends, or emissaries of God. Call us loving energy, angels or guides. Beneath, before, within … impregnating, inviting.

When you place your hands over your heart and breathe, you may feel none of these things. There may be sadness, doubt, anger, or simply coldness. Allow these things. Bring them the warmth of your touch. Hold them against your heart.

We will tell you a secret now: if you allow the smallest bit of love into these forsaken places, it is as if you have been touched by the hand of God. All God wants is the loving. Here is the answer to everything: separation, fear, loneliness, war, anger … all the suffering of the earth and its inhabitants. The simplest gesture of love is the answer. Just this one. Because you are the Beloved. The Beloved is yourself. You are never alone. The whole of creation is held in your hands, learning to love a little bit, just this moment. That is all, really. It is so simple.

This will not make sense to your mind. It is as if Humpty-Dumpty has fallen and the mind was long ago irreparably confused. *Stop trying to fix it! Let it go. Try it now this way—the way we have been showing you. The other way hasn't been working so well.*

What do we say to all the war and suffering of this planet?

Peace is even now blooming within each heart so subtly you will not know it. Do not drain your energy in opposition. Do not divert your most powerful assets in anger or fear. Redirect. Go deep. Find the compassion for the self, for the other, and for this world. Mine for the true gold and bring it out of its hiding places.

What does it mean, to mine for gold? How does this translate to the people who will be looking for concrete answers?

Welcome everything with love. Love produces the alchemy always, without fail. Find the most violent criminal and nourish him with love. Do not do anything. Hold him in your heart. Focus love and focus love again. Your heart is like a forge—the only forge on earth powerful enough to turn base metals into gold. This is your unfailing asset. Use it for everything. Any negative circumstance can be transformed by love. Take a violent scenario in a distant land and hold it inwardly as if it were a crying child. House and soothe it in your heart. Learn to be the mother of everything. This is the blessed transformation. It is a forgotten art in most places, this kind alchemy. Now materialism praises all that glitters, however base the metal and however temporary the form. The gold that we are speaking of is eternal and imperishable. It is also known as the Living Water that satisfies the thirst of the soul forever.

It is still hard to believe that such an obscure sounding thing would be enough for facing down the violence and suffering of this age.

We can agree that a new element is needed in the global picture. It may feel generic to say that the new element is Love. Let's be more specific. It is Universal Consciousness, a true awareness that what is done to you in a harmful way is harmful to me. What is helpful to you helps me. But what will make this sort of shift possible? How is this change in awareness to occur? For this to occur a new ingredient is required, a new development in enlightenment is in order. It is the understanding of the true eternal nature of reality.

It is the "Aha" moment when a leader will realize that no useful and lasting power can be achieved through force or domination. And it is the moment when the people will know that they cannot be dominated by any outside force.

This kind of knowing has eluded civilizations, by and large, for thousands of years. But the enlightened individuals have understood—Gandhi, Sojourner Truth, Martin Luther King.... They experienced a mighty truth within themselves that could then be applied to global situations. But the knowing began within: the forging of a force invincible because it was born of immortal elements. This is the alchemy we are speaking of. Let us mine for the gold that does not perish.

And so we advocate turning inward and beginning with earnest efforts at self-love. This is a challenging frontier—perhaps the most vital one of all. Do not imagine that it will be easy. It may be the work of a lifetime. Begin now. Begin gently. Know that there is great encouragement in unseen realms, for this is the work of this moment.

It seems to me that all of the inspired, enlightened individuals of history have always tried for this ... how is this time different?

In this time the material human frontiers are imperiled. What has been the work of the few becomes the imperative of the collective. The time is at hand for humanity to shift on a vast scale.

I see. There is nowhere else to go, and the time is short for our lifestyle to survive on earth.

The time is now.

So this is my work: this conversation?

This is your daily work: spinning straw into gold. Others are joining in this work, and you may begin to feel them as if you worked all together as energy transformers, weaving out of mortal material a finer fabric. Think of this as the new industry of the 21st Century: the Great Alchemy. You have no idea how many beings are engaged in this work.

And, by the way, if your dreams of darkness and the resulting depressive moods drive you deeper into this magnificent work, might you not be grateful even for these, as if you were rushing to bring light out of threatening storm clouds? It is no small thing, this Alchemy. To bring light out of darkness is the greatest magic of all. It is God's work.

The Vessel

As I sit in silence this morning hoping for help from unseen companions, I am aware of heaviness and self-judgment.

We are here. We are always grateful for the opportunity to share time with you in love and we are grateful for your willingness to offer yourself as a channel for healing guidance for yourself and the collective.

My 'vessel' feels most impure and unworthy today.

The purity or worth of the vessel is not the point—it is the willingness to be an offering. This is all that is ever asked or required. Please understand that as soon as you invite us in we cleanse the frequency completely: this is part of our offering to you. Our presence increases the frequency of Divine Light, not only here in your heart and body, but also within this home, and on this earth plane. Every time you offer yourself and say, "Come," the holy work occurs—every time without exception.

Of course, this is simple but not easy work. The world of humanity is charged with difficulty. But the enlightened eye can see in every difficulty an opportunity, and here the smile of remembrance comes: every obstacle is an opportunity for grace. An obstacle, lovingly attended, can become a doorway to great beauty.

There is something we wish to emphasize now. You have a tendency towards negative self-analysis—the cup is half empty. What is required is no self-analysis—none. Your mind has no measuring tools for this spiritual work which is your calling. No soul is worthy; none is unworthy. Stop thinking that by self-analysis you can make an iota of improvement. You cannot.

Breathe in, breathe out. Apart from that—and the upkeep of body and home—there is little you need to do. Remember when, in afterlife, your father observed that so little he had concerned himself about in his life was of any real importance? Consider the mystery that surrounds you in life: there are times of joy and sorrow over which you have little control … times of grace and times of upheaval. There are baffling cosmic mysteries and miracles of creation. There is life … death … eternity. Do you understand these things?

The part of life over which you have control is very small indeed: "I may love in this moment, or I may not love." That is about all. Love or not love. In this part of the human dream the illusion of control is almost megalomaniacal. Your body is a small actor on a great stage. And in some ways this is a great relief. Let God be great. And align yourself with that greatness: do its work and receive its benefits. Serve and delight in God's presence. But do not torture yourself with delusions of individual power. No power exists apart from Source (the generator, if you will) and there is freedom in remembering this. Align with Source and then relax. The rest will follow.

For the reader:

Take a few moments to breathe and ask yourself: "How might I rest in this moment? What temporal concerns can I release into the sweet river of acceptance and joy?" We are being reminded that offering ourselves to receive divine Love is our highest calling in these tumultuous times.

Love's energy is transforming this earth, one heart at a time. Our job is to let it in to this one heart. Divine energy will do the rest, if we are willing. Ask yourself: "Am I willing?"

As you offer your deepest feelings in these pages or your journal, you are increasing the flow of divine discourse, not only in your private spaces, but also within the Collective. Please do not underestimate the time you spend in this conversation—it is a vital work.

... Ask yourself: "Am I willing?" As you offer your deepest feelings in these pages or your journal, you are increasing the flow of divine discourse, not only in your private spaces, but also within the Collective.

... Ask yourself: "Am I willing?" As you offer your deepest feelings in these pages or your journal, you are increasing the flow of divine discourse, not only in your private spaces, but also within the Collective.

FORGIVING THE DREAM

"Your wounds of love can only heal
When you can forgive this dream."
—Hafiz

The illusions of this material life are so persuasive. In one moment there may be ecstatic joy, and in the next unbearable sorrow. Sometimes it feels that the burden of mortality is too hard to bear.

Banished Sorrow

How can I forgive this dream? Sometimes it seems that sorrow is seeping through the cracks … the dam is crumbling and tidal waves of pain and loss are pushing back my efforts of love and hope. I know better. My spirit knows that love is the song that lasts forever and suffering is temporary, but how do I forgive this dream?

This is a difficult path. This human life is a difficult path. From an eternal perspective we call these passages dreams but for the human heart they are unspeakably real. The abuse of innocence, vast suffering … death.

What does it mean to forgive these things?

Begin by holding them tenderly, even if they break your heart. Allow this heart to be bathed in grief: there is no stopping it in any case. There is no escape. It will do you no harm. Notice that something else begins to envelope you: a great calm. This is "the Peace that passes understanding."

Remember that this culture has attempted to abolish grief and frailty. And so at this crucial moment of healing and awakening there will be waves of banished sorrow. They will not harm you. Like lost children they seek safe haven. Allow them to come: this is a kindness. Even if the sorrows are not your own, accept them anyway as they are seeking healing. This is not an idle exercise. Energy is shifting now on a vast scale. Institutions, powers and policies that have held dominion for thousands of years are toppling. The energies that supported these structures are breaking off in all directions. They will need shelter while they find their way. So welcome them all. This will lend goodness to chaotic times and fertilize the positive changes to come.

For myself, at a personal level, there are things I can't seem to forgive. And outside my window this morning I've seen three military carriers in the sky … (going to Afghanistan?) How can I forgive this dream?

They are doing the best they can. And this is also the sorrow. This is the best they can do. "Forgive them, for they know not what they do:" Jesus asked God to forgive his murderers.

How much sorrow can one person bear?

We are not asking you to take on more than you are able, only to be human. This human being is a great creation who can suffer for others and carry their pain. And this is the divine love they offer.

Such a strange and awesome journey: what is the meaning of it all?

Someday you will understand. Someday you will "see face to face." Today you are bearing something, and this is no idle task. To bear is to tend and help birth. You are birthing new worlds in this sweet offering of sorrow.

There are so many good people in the world ... people who offer themselves over and over with steadfast kindness and faith.

Yes.

Have they forgiven the dream? Have they risen from their bed of heartache to bear a new world?

There is need in this time for rest and replenishment. And we want to say that it should be pleasurable and fun. This is the part we wish for you to playfully explore.

We also want to say that it is time to stop underestimating your work in this planetary moment. There is no measurement for it in the crumbling materialistic super-culture that cries out: "Save me from myself!"

Your minds cannot grasp what is now taking place. Only deep attunement will take you to the great veins of hope that herald new life forms. The modern mind, lacking eternal vision, sees every death as final and tragic, where deeper attunements afford glimpses of exciting new developments.

We suggest that you do not try to understand with your conditioned mental perceptions, as this mind itself is part of what is being replaced. These minds, in the so-called First World, have been taught the practice of human domination over nature and other humans. They have been schooled on the heroic exploits of a series vanquishers of indigenous civilizations. These minds have been conditioned to accept the assumption that arsenals of mass murder are necessary to protect a superior life-style. And, perhaps most tragically, these minds have been encouraged to avoid the painful parts of human life through a glut of material pleasure and the objectification of what is unpleasant.

Perhaps it is time for this relic of a mind to be retired. A new earth requires new tenderness, sensitivity and vulnerability. So let go of all that is dying, and remember that a deep and sweet awakening is heralding unimaginable harmony, innovation and joy.

All will be well.

Eternal Consciousness

I found it difficult to regain my place of peace in you following a troubling news report. I know that this conversation is all that is eternal, and it is light-filled and loving. But the tragedies of this world—however temporal—are profoundly distressing.

Will you speak to me about these times? What guidance is there for us? I sense that our material perception of reality is shifting. And one can dwell on this disruption or begin to align with nascent frequencies.

We are here, dear one. These 'nascent frequencies' are growing stronger and are more available. It is increasingly easy for people to tune in and receive messages of love and truth. Whatever passage they choose, with a pure heart, will be fruitful. Our companionship and guidance will be increasingly apparent, and new vision will be granted for the way of the present and future. Indeed there is no present or future—all time is now. This perception of the eternal, present moment will increase as material phenomena reveal their transparency.

For the reader, then, the 'work' is to step back and find a space of present moment throughout the day, especially when confronted with challenging situations. And they must understand that this present awareness is eternal. This awareness is the unceasing conscious life. If there were to be a sudden interruption of the body's function—accident or death—this consciousness would continue.

In human evolution this eternal consciousness is the next form of being. In time it will be uninterrupted by material preoccupation. Although exciting innovations will continue to occur, the foundation of being will have shifted out of identification with material life. This is difficult for the mind to conceive at present, and so many teachers and guides are assisting, visibly as well as invisibly. The seeker need never despair. There are many doorways into the joy and freedom of eternal awareness. Each reader will find these words affirmed as they ingest them, and allow the signs and messages to come.

The Veils Are Thin

I know that many who have physically died for brief periods and returned have spoken of similar near-death phenomena: light, a loving presence, the viewing of their distressed body from a detached distance. Is this a glimpse of what we are speaking about in the sense that each of us can experience that distance from the body *now*—the presence of divine light and the absence of mortal distress?

Yes. This is the possibility we are addressing in this time. It can be said that "the veils are thin," and this eternal perspective is increasingly available. Life can feel more fluid in this sense.

The toppling of material systems runs parallel to a changing molecular quality. Scientists will one day identify this evolution. But for each one of you what is important to know is that relaxing your grip on what your minds perceive as reality will allow grace to lighten the mortal load. This has been a very heavy load. But consider the possibility that even what has manifested itself as evil in human history has always been an attempt—however ill-advised—to shoulder this burden.

And now myriad counselors come to lift the load—not individually and sequentially, as in times past—but everywhere at once. It might be said that all the seers, angels, prophets and helpers are united in this universal birthing.

Even as the labor pangs of a woman in childbirth come in increasingly intense waves, this 'contraction' is reaching its apex and great assistance is at hand for the cosmic birthing. But, yes, there will be pain. And for each individual it will be helpful to tune in to the ever-present assistance. Each of you will experience this birthing at an individual level, and it will at times be frightening. The gentle and wise midwives, close at hand, wish to wipe your brow and praise your great efforts, for you are birthing not only your own great liberation, but also the joyful expansion of all who will follow.

All of this requires the space and time to be still enough to listen. We are so close you can hear our heartbeats. As you hear our comforting voices, praising you for the great courage to be human in this time, you will relax and release tension, separation and fear. We will take care of the rest.

For the Reader:

In your life there are birth pangs: something is dying and something new is emerging. There may be specific sorrow, fear or anxiety. It will be helpful to write what you are feeling with the voice of your heart. This simple expression will open the pathways for spiritual communication.

Take a few quiet moments to write how you feel and to ask for guidance. Divine companions are waiting to offer wisdom and love.

... In your life there are birth pangs: something is dying and something new is emerging. Take a few quiet moments to write how you feel and to ask for guidance. Divine companions are waiting to offer wisdom and love.

... In your life there are birth pangs: something is dying and something new is emerging. Take a few quiet moments to write how you feel and to ask for guidance. Divine companions are waiting to offer wisdom and love.

THAT'S HOW THE LIGHT GETS IN

"Ring the bells that still can ring / Forget your Perfect Offering
There is a crack, a crack in everything
That's how the light gets in...."
—Leonard Cohen, *Anthem*

Environmental, political and economic disasters fill the news of the day. Some consider that we are living in the End Times, and some refer to ancient indigenous prophecies of the dawning of a New Age. "What is Truth?" as Pontius Pilate famously asked. What is the divine perspective?

The Individual Heart and the Universal Heart Are One

Speak to me, Beloved, about these times—the wars, earthquakes, tsunamis … the atomic disasters, domestic violence, genocide. Speak to me about the possibility that I have misperceived all of this. Open my eyes (if only for a moment) to the truth of it.

We are here, dear one. Is it enough to know that these questions are beyond the scope of your vision, your mental capacity to grasp?

All upheaval and violence—the atrocities beyond bearing—all are somehow in their secret core a face of love. How do we know this? Because every soul is on an eternal trajectory. Some come forth in primitive forms, but even these can be teachers. How can we say these things to the broken-hearted victims of violence? Because we are with them in the incomprehensibility of rape and genocide. We are holding their hearts through abandonment and grief.

There are so many doorways to Love, and each one of you is bound to find it. The wounded will be healed, the broken made whole. Angels, guides, spirits of all forms are ever at work to transform all of this.

It is a hard and often a brutal school. Why does such a place exist in a universe inspired by love? Imagine molten lava, fiery fluid. Imagine the blinding storm that levels everything ... the destruction of cities and lifestyles ... the breaking heart of individual consciousness—that agony of separation. The story of mankind is not the rise and fall of kingdoms, but rather the dismembering of the soul.

What are you trying to say?

We are trying to say what you cannot quite hear....

History is not the material phenomena. There is an unbroken progression in the evolution of the heart. It has never been more bright or strong or even more hopeful. Its weakness has been burning away in the fierce furnace of history—the dross that kept the purity at bay, and all that threatened to pollute it from within. In the fiery explosion of the thousand forms we are witnessing the birth of a universal heart of Love.

It is here, like the buds of spring, the shoots secretly peeking through the detritus of the long winter. Content yourself with searching for those new signs of life, for they are everywhere. A new world is at hand that could not coexist with dying forms.

Rub your eyes and shed your pessimism. Be like a child expecting to be surprised by tiny miracles shooting up everywhere. And be dazzled when they appear. This is the time we have all fought for these thousands of years. Awakening is at hand. The fields have been cleared by fire. Hearts have been purified by the hot furnaces of devotion. Allow your mind's perceptions to rest. The time of awakening has arrived.

What you can do

By allowing your own personal space to be open to divine love you are doing a great work. The battle of "principalities and powers in high places" is really over this: Will the human heart succumb to Love?

The battle is not 'out there.' It is here within each heart. Self-love is the most difficult portal to open precisely because it is the most important. Look at the story of Job. Would he love—even in the face of direst adversity—or would he succumb to faithless bitterness? The question is: does Love sit on the throne of the human being? And this begins with the love of self, because the self is of divine substance.

The way the alchemy works is difficult to describe. Love must occupy the human sphere: this is the great frontier. With material logic you mistakenly assume that one human heart is small, as one person seems like a drop in the great ocean of humanity. We wish to tell you that each heart is a vast realm and that nothing is more important than the work of a divine soul. Imagine the expanse of eternity (if you can!) One heart can be an eternal Light, casting its rays forever in all directions. Any act or expression of Love introduces invincible power into many realms.

Imagine introducing a powerfully toxic element into a body of water: all the fish will die, along with plant-forms and microscopic algae. Now imagine one agent so powerful it can heal all the life-forms, not only in this moment, but into the future forever. Such is the power of divine Love introduced into the human heart. That heart, existing within the sea of humanity, can transform the whole. Begin to believe this, dear one. Begin to let the scales fall from your eyes and perceive what is True.

You may repeat to yourself over and over the simple words, "I Am Love." More powerful than any atomic explosion is the force of divine Love within one human heart. The individual heart and the Universal Heart are one.

For the Reader:

As a final exercise, we ask you to envision light and hope emerging from every place of darkness and dissolution. Just envision it: Light everywhere. Global transformation. Tell yourself: "This is possible. This I believe. All things are possible with God." At the end of the day—at the end of your life—you will discover the truth of this. You will emerge from this difficult school of human existence and find yourself surrounded by infinite Love. The very good news is that every day you can enter into this beautiful realm by holding close to the Source of love and eternal bliss.

Try the exercise of repeating to yourself: "*I Am Love.*" Write the words in the space below, and attune to them with your whole being. It will help to record whatever obstacles or questions arise, and ask the voice of gentle compassion to speak....

... Try the exercise of repeating to yourself: "I Am Love." Write the words in the space below, and attune to them with your whole being.
It will help to record whatever obstacles or questions arise, and ask the voice of gentle compassion to speak....

... Try the exercise of repeating to yourself: "I Am Love." Write the words in the space below, and attune to them with your whole being.
It will help to record whatever obstacles or questions arise, and ask the voice of gentle compassion to speak....

HOSTING A LISTENING CIRCLE

We are all aware that great change is upon us. Top-heavy systems are crumbling and making way for local, collective solutions. People are gathering regionally to ask: how can we find sufficiency here … what can we create within this community? This impulse is echoed within the spiritual dimensions of our being. Dysfunction has left us feeling isolated and adrift within systems that do not sustain us. We are seeking new sustenance for the soul.

The listening circle is a wonderful way to explore and deepen our practice of opening to loving guidance in these times of intense global and personal change. Here we are encouraged to lay down the burdens that prevent us from accepting the love of the universe as well as the joy of communion with our visible community. It is beautifully described in the following message I received in meditation:

The Golden Community

The listening circle supports a new frequency. Springing up all over, these pockets of receptivity assist us in attuning to the gracious frequencies that form the awakened global consciousness: the Golden Community. This is the next step in human evolution. Heed it well.

It is not a question of the leader teaching something s/he knows and the others do not. Rather, it is a space for evolving all together in this experience we are being offered of greater unity with Source, or the Beloved. Feel and cultivate this new internal sensation as you learn to release outdated forms of mind and ego which no longer serve you.

The work of the Golden Community can be nurtured anytime, anywhere. When you are alone you may ask: "What is the voice of Love saying to me now?" When you are in groups you will experience the encouragement of the collective and you may feel waves of understanding as the new form reveals itself within the circle.

Practice self-love. Ground the frequency. Simplify your systems. Lay low. Listen.

... listen some more. Know that all is well in the great eternal energy of Love.

Practicing self-love and simplicity within the empathic community expands the frequency. We no longer look to the prevailing culture for the quality and form of our being. We no longer listen to the harsh internal or external critics. We no longer buy into the systems of self-centeredness, isolation, fear and greed that have dominated human history. Suspending judgment in any form we ask: "What does the lover of my soul have to say today? What am I here to understand as I listen?"

The embodiment of new consciousness requires new forms. The listening circle is one such form. As if we were in a classroom for spirit, we are here to receive guidance, but there is no visible teacher. We are here to be transformed, healed, schooled in new ways through the simple act of listening with new senses, hearing with new ears. That seems mysterious, but so does the butterfly who emerges from the caterpillar's shroud. We are being transformed within the chrysalis of the old life. And the Divine Alchemist is the teacher.

Preparation

It is important to keep in mind that hosting a listening circle is a source of joy. Let this thought guide you as offer space and opportunity for others to come together and share in this journey. It is as if we have all been invited to a party to celebrate the great spiritual awakening, and the host's job is simply to prepare a safe and welcoming space. There is no need to be special or worthy or good. Every listening circle will be different and unique. The only real formula is the careful offering of space, time and intention. At the beginning it is helpful to have clear structure, but as the group evolves new patterns will emerge. Remember that we are on a frontier of consciousness where anything may happen.

First, of course, you will invite those who might be interested, briefly describing the nature of the circles and reminding them to bring a journal or paper and pen. It may take a while to find the best time for most people, but these logistics will work themselves out. Recalling that the heaviness of the human condition often carries fear, discouragement, and other burdensome energies, let the space of your gathering be made light and welcoming through the use of sage or flowers, candles, pillows or blankets. Your positive intentions will say to your guests: "Welcome: here is a safe place of kindness and nurture." The smallest gesture on you part will be multiplied by the loving energies you are allowing. This is not *your* group, after all: you are simply serving at the spiritual banquet, and many are hungry. So do not doubt or worry: as you offer this gift of time and space the energies of Love and Light will do their work, so greet each guest with humility and a smile. Remember that all will be well.

Structure

After warm greetings we open the circle with a few moments of silence where we begin to imagine the presence of unseen helpers. As always, language is a question. What are we speaking of when we use words like Source, the Lover, God, Allah, Yahweh? Can we be sure of the nature of Angels, Guides, or even Ancestors? I have tried to be inclusive and humble: who are we, after all, to name the creative pulse of the universe? We are inviting this unnameable presence in an atmosphere of openness and safety, holding one another with care. We are riding a new wave here. This process is outside of the realm of ordinary social discourse, and will have a different rhythm and frequency. Spaces of silence are often the most powerful element in the gathering.

I usually follow the initial silence by speaking of my pleasure in the gathering and sharing excitement about recent thoughts or guidance I've received, then by giving a brief overview of how the time will go. At this point in our evolution, the monthly circle that gathers in my home lasts for about two and a half hours. Following my introduction, we go around the circle, and each person may say her/his name and briefly what has brought him here today. (In subsequent gatherings this time may be used for 'checking in' in whatever way feels useful.) I try to model attentive listening and respect, and mention can be made of the need for confidentiality. This listening circle will not be a time for general conversation— we are carefully tuning in to deeper frequencies and aiding one another in acceptance and appreciation. To comment on what others have expressed or to offer suggestions is not usually helpful.

In the beginning, you will wish to speak of how to enter into this new form of listening, and encourage your guests to be patient with themselves: "Remember that we have all the time in the world to enter into divine conversation, so relax and open yourself to unseen frequencies until the loving one comes. You might imagine that you are inwardly turning a radio dial, trying on different channels until you find the one that is gentle and merciful. Do not expect thunder and a voice from on high. These messages may come like fleeting impressions at first. You may think that you are making them up. Don't concern yourself with that: just receive what comes." Initially some people find it daunting to listen for a spiritual voice. In this case I have asked them to imagine the voice of a loving friend or compassionate parent.

An inspiring quote or passage is sometimes helpful for the collective attunement of the group. I often use a passage from this book, or choose another source. I love the excerpt from a poem by the Persian Sufi mystic, Hafiz:

"For God to make love, for the divine alchemy to work,
The pitcher needs a still cup.
Why ask Hafiz to say anything more about your most vital requirement?"

Exercises

In our gatherings there is usually time for two listening exercises, each followed by some space for those who wish to share their experience. We begin by centering ourselves in awareness of our emotions and asking a question or seeking particular guidance, and then we listen for the voice of Love. Early in the process we would listen for eight or ten minutes, but lately the deliciousness of this space calls for more time, and we are allowing about 20-30 minutes. You will enjoy experimenting together to find what feels good within the circle.

Initially you may use guidance like the example below, to help your guests center themselves in relaxation:

"Sit or lie down comfortably. In this time of stillness, be in this present moment. Notice the sounds... Breathe gently into your chest and then into your belly. Take a series of deep, relaxed breaths. Now begin to notice your own feelings: are you comfortable? Your thoughts: are you here? Your heart: what is the state of your heart? If it is useful, place your hand over your heart. Allow your breath to come and go. We will take some time here in relaxation and gentle nurture. Remember, when you feel your internal mental chatter is in the way, that this, too, can be observed and loved. As soon as you observe, the chatter becomes somewhat akin to the traffic noise or birdsong—part of your environment. Practice adopting the stance of observer and returning to your breath."

In early gatherings I used the exercise on page 5 of this book, reading it aloud and asking the group to take five or six minutes to internalize the question: "What am I seeking with all my heart?" For many it is helpful to record the direction of their thoughts. Then I might say: "Now I am asking you to experience the presence of Love in this room. Imagine that this love is surrounding you in the form of guides, angels, divine messengers, ancestors. Remember, through all of your pains and sorrows, all of your joys and victories, the lover of your soul is embracing you and saying, 'You have done so well, my dear one. It is not easy to be human. I love you.'" Choose your own words, or you may use the direction on page 119.

Ask your group to take a few moments to feel the presence of this love, for it is real. Your body will one day disintegrate, but this relationship between you and the source of love will continue forever. Allow this love: breathe it in and rest in it. You are not asking with your mind. Wait until it is your heart that begins to receive the voice of Love. It may take the form of a feeling, an image, or a message. If there are any words for you, you may record them, or just remain in the place of this experience. Receive it all in gratitude.

At the end of our appointed time of silence, I ring a little bell and—after allowing a bit more appreciative silence—begin by asking: "Is there anyone who would like to share what they have written or received?" When someone seems to have experienced a sensation or a message from the voice of Love, I might ask them, "How does this *feel?*" Remind them that this sharing is a helpful encouragement to the circle, but not necessary. If someone wishes to pass, it is perfectly all right.

For the second meditation you may use another exercise in the book, or choose a direction that feels right to you. "What are your worries? What are you seeking? Where do you need guidance? What are your concerns for the world?" All these are questions that may be posed in the simple format of seeking the voice and viewpoint of eternal Love. (In our small group we have found that the question "Who am I?" can open up a wealth of meditative experience.) As you listen, gradually patterns will emerge that will be new to your internal cosmology. "I am enough. I am loved. I am eternally safe." You may hear hope and light expressed for the future of this world. The voice of Love has many healing words to offer, as well as deep wisdom and endless compassion.

As you progress in the path of your circles, you will be shown the way. You will be able to feel into the timing. Checking in with your spiritual source as the meeting times approach, you will learn to hold and guide the circle with increasing ease.

I wish you joy on your sacred journey ~
with blessings, grace and gratitude,

Jane Smith Bernhardt

Jane Smith Bernhardt is a writer, spiritual director, actress and portrait artist who has traveled extensively with her visual art exhibits, original solo dramatic performances and inspirational talks. In places as scarred as Auschwitz and Hiroshima, her passion has been to awaken our hearts to the possibility of loving global consciousness.

A graduate of the two-year *Guild for Spiritual Guidance*, she also completed a seven-year course in multi-dimensional healing through Greta Bro's *Wisdom Ways Mystery School*. Years of preparation in spiritual listening have helped Jane explore the mystery of death itself, which can awaken both our greatest fears and our most inspiring possibilities. Receiving messages from her father after his death, Jane shared their extraordinary journey in her first book, *We Are Here: love never dies*.

In this exciting moment of human evolution, more and more people are opening to spiritual dialogue. In her second book, *The Sweet Conversation: a guide to spiritual listening*, Jane shares the inspiring messages she has recorded from unseen guidance, and offers simple exercises for the reader to experience this transformative conversation.

Soon we may form an internet site for sharing cherished messages and experiences.
To stay updated please visit:

www.janebernhardt.com   janesb@comcast.net

CPSIA information can be obtained
at www.ICGtesting.com
Printed in the USA
FFOW01n1450120217
32253FF